FILL YOUR GLASS WITH GOLD

When It's Half-Full or Even Completely Shattered

Written by Hillary Saffran

Illustration and Design by

YoungJu Kim

ISBN: 9798218193119

Written by Hillary Saffran

Illustration and Design by YoungJu Kim

Table of Contents

Table of Contents

YOU ARE HERE.

For a reason.

Something has happened in your life to bring you to this place at this time.

Unfortunate things happen to us at times because that's the experience of life, which is full of events, both happy and sad.

So, if you have experienced any adversity lately, I'd like to share with you an art form that is beautifully symbolic of the joy and the sorrow in life, especially when the pottery of your life has cracks, which is common to us all.

KINTSUGI

What is *kintsugi*? It's a way of turning broken pottery into works of art.

Some four or five centuries ago in Japan, a lavish technique emerged for repairing broken ceramics. Artisans began using lacquer and gold pigment to put shattered vessels back together. This tradition — known as *kintsugi*, meaning "golden seams" (or *kintsukuroi*, "golden repair") — is still going strong.

For the Japanese, kintsugi is part of a broader philosophy of embracing the beauty of human flaws. I see it as even more than that: finding the hidden beauty in adversity and turning it into something of extreme value and meaning. It's the art of turning the broken pottery of your life into pure gold.

The next time you encounter a difficult obstacle or problem, you should smile and say, "Here's my chance to grow."

- Zig Ziglar [1]

You, the reader, may say, *"The last thing I need is some flowery quote. You have no idea how I got here and how bad I feel. You can take your quotes and . . ."*

My response would be, "Alright, alright. All I'm saying is that at some time we've all had regrets and have felt bad about what we've done, or said, and then we suffered the consequences. We've all had 'Oh no-second!' moments."

'Oh no-second! moments?'

Yes, that second, that moment that you realize you made a mistake that you can't undo.

Did you ever hit send on an email and then you instantly regretted it? Or said something that you thought was funny, but it came out totally wrong and you knew that it was misconstrued, but you didn't address it right away and you felt bad about it every time you saw that person or even thought about it, and you beat yourself up for the next five years over it?

Yup.

----

[1] "Zig Ziglar quotes," AZ Quotes, accessed March 15, 2023, https://www.azquotes.com/author/16182-Zig

Well, I have, too. I get it, and that's why I'm sharing this with you now.

Okay, go on.

How you respond to adversity can affect your life in a negative way, or it can truly transform your life for the better and help many others also. I have thought about this often in my work in social services, where I've been a case manager for public assistance clients. Many of these clients experienced tragedy, which is why they applied for welfare to begin with.

This book was born from a workshop that I created for my clients called "Your Path to Progress," which relays success stories of several historical figures as well as people in entertainment, business, science, and more who overcame huge obstacles to achieve great accomplishments that serve humanity. I wanted to give my clients hope and convey that they were responsible for their lives and choices—that they can be victorious overcomers, not victims, and that they can respond to their circumstances in positive and empowering ways.

In this book, I have written my own story and those of historical and well-known figures. Other stories were contributed by friends and family.

I often tell my clients, **"Whatever you have gone through or are going through now—no matter how difficult it seems—it will be useful for you in the future. Out of great difficulty many have created non-profits, formed ministries, and have gathered more skill sets for a new or better career."**

For example, in countless communities all over the world, organizations have been formed because of:

Domestic violence

Homelessness

Addiction recovery

Hunger

Medical help

Job training

Transitional housing out of rehab and incarceration

Death due to drunk drivers

Everything you can imagine.

It is my hope that you will find hope from the stories in this book and that you will learn to turn any adversity you may have experienced into your own pure gold.

A Man is Not a Plan

I was born in Brooklyn, New York, more than forty-five years ago (okay, maybe fifty-five plus), and I had dreams like many other women of my generation. You graduate high school, you go to college, you get a job, you get married, you have children, you have grandchildren, you retire to the "promised land" (Florida), and then you die.

Well, life didn't turn out like I thought it would. My mother died when I was seven, leaving my father, myself, and my older brother. My father remarried soon after, and I inherited a stepmother and older stepbrother, but alas, we were not the Brady Bunch. More like a Long Island version of *Mommy Dearest*. My family took the word "fun" out of "dysfunctional."

I moved out before I graduated high school, rented a room, and worked to support myself. I put myself through college, then moved to Manhattan after graduation for a series of jobs. I had been a theater and journalism major in college, and now I was in the Big Apple with big dreams and very little confidence in myself. I worked a series of office jobs and took some vocal lessons because I loved to sing and had some head shots taken for commercials, but I found myself adrift and basically emotionally unhealed, going nowhere.

Things had not gotten better with my family—I had lost touch for several years as things were very painful with those relationships. My parents had made sure that my brothers did not invite me to their weddings, and both brothers, being four years older than myself, had never taken on the "big brother" role anyway. We were always distant from each other. I found out from a neighborhood friend's mother that my parents had moved to Florida from Long Island—three years earlier.

I felt so lonely in New York. You could walk down the street amidst thousands of people and feel completely alone. At one of my jobs, I made friends with a gal that wanted to go to Seattle. I thought, "Why not? I have nothing here."

We drove to Seattle. I needed a job, and I got one working for a man who was from Brooklyn—who knew! He had his own refrigeration and appliance repair business, and I was the dispatcher. Carl didn't tell me his real age, that he was not fully divorced, and that he had six children when he took such a shine to me.

I didn't know what the terms "twenty-six-year-old rebound" and "trophy wife" meant when Carl asked me to marry him. I knew that he was like a father figure, but after I moved in with him before we got married, I was too emotionally entwined to get out. We went to California to get married, lived there for two years, and came back to Seattle, where I briefly became a stepmother to two of his daughters. His oldest child was two years younger than me. It was like a bad Danielle Steel novel.

We had a beautiful son, but the marriage ended when I finally took myself to counseling and things escalated in an unhealthy way with Carl. I was losing my fear of my husband's temper and was becoming more confident in myself. Carl blamed the counselor for our divorce. Now I was a single mom of a twenty-two-month-old child, fully responsible for our financial well-being as child support was iffy.

To be with my son, I became a preschool teacher, but it was never enough money. I frequently read the want ads in the paper until one day, I saw an ad in the *Seattle Times*: "Be a Clown, Will Train." This really resonated with me because of my love for theatre in high school and college. That little ad was a life changer. I ended up clowning for twenty-eight years for extra income. It was fabulous; you make $100 an hour and keep your clothes on!

I needed clown business cards, so I walked into a print shop one day and a nice-looking guy at the counter took an interest in me. It was one of the first times that I'm sure I heard the voice of God in my head: "Leave him alone—he's a nut." True to form, I ignored that huge red flag, and we were soon engaged. Steve had an obsession to go to Alaska, which was never an obsession of mine.

But in the endless quest to find Mr. Wrong, I soon followed Steve to Anchorage, Alaska, where he left me and my son high and dry. My things were in storage, except for my clown suitcase and some other valuables, so I walked into a pawn shop one day in search of a guitar to use for birthday parties to make some extra money aside from my job at a hotel.

The guy who sold me the guitar, Scott, was enamored with me, and before you know it, he started showering me with jewelry (from the pawn shop, of course). One of these jewels was an engagement ring. You think I would have acknowledged the red flags, but alas, I didn't know what he meant by the statement, "I have fifty-nine days." (It meant days of sobriety.) Scott did tell me early on, "If you live in Alaska for more than five years and leave, you will end up coming back."

Now I was married for the second time, but I had never lived with an alcoholic and drug addict before. Two babies and four and a half years later, with my son now eight years old, I wanted to die because another divorce loomed soon. Here I was, with a college degree, work experience, two failed marriages, three children, and now on welfare.

Where was the course Standards 101 in college?

At one point, I got in touch with my parents again. During my divorce, my father said, "You sure could pick 'em!"

Seven months after the divorce, I met a man who was a friend of a friend of mine. He was an airplane mechanic who owned his own Super Cub. An airplane guy is loads of fun. My kids loved him, I loved him, but it was an on-again, off-again relationship between his divorce scars and mine.

I couldn't stand it anymore after several years of relationship ups and downs, though I had become friends with his sister in Colorado. I had also met another guy on the rebound who I now refer to as Mr. Really Wrong, who had an obsession to leave Alaska and go to Colorado. I thought I needed a change after twelve years in Anchorage, so I moved to Colorado, where I worked in the employment field and learned ventriloquism to add to my clowning.

I had many bad dating experiences, and Alaska Airplane Guy was not completely out of the picture as he could not totally let go (and neither could I). Then, I was laid off after living seven years in Colorado, and I also found my youngest daughter, then fifteen, dating a boy much older than her.

What a perfect time to go back to Alaska! I decided to come to the Mat-Su Valley, where I discovered that Airplane Guy had been seriously dating someone for some time, which he had failed to reveal on his visits to Colorado and in his phone calls. But that was okay because I finally learned that "a man is not a plan."

I became involved in the local arts community and met many wonderful people. One day I saw an ad in our local community paper for an audition for Alaska Home Companion. This was for the Valley Arts Alliance, made up of many fabulous women of a similar age. We all became great friends.

When my youngest daughter graduated high school and wanted to go back to Denver, I thought of going with her. My new friends said, "No, stay here." Most of my friends are happily married women. I asked them to pull my arm, and they gladly did. So, I stayed. I bought a beautiful home in Palmer in the picturesque Matanuska–Susitna Valley. It is my cottage in the woods.

Hmm . . . where's your happy ending? Are you still single and scarred from men to this day? What's the gold in your cup?!

I did meet someone special when I turned sixty-two, nine years after I came back to Alaska from Colorado. We got married a year after we met. It is the happiest and healthiest relationship I have ever been in.

Now one of the ironies of my life is that my job in social services is finding employment for mostly women who thought that a man was a plan, but the dream shattered, and they find themselves on welfare. I get them jobs to get them off welfare.

So, if life does not turn out like you thought it would, that's okay. That happened to me when I took a long, winding thirty-five-year road to Alaska, where friends became my family, and I finally came home.

I've been working "on the other side of the desk" for the past two decades now and feel that I am a much better case manager and employment specialist because of what I've learned in my own journey and welfare experience. I empower my clients to become self-sufficient as soon as possible, and they know that they've acquired an authentic cheerleader to help them on their way.

I even completed training to become a transformational coach and therapist in my own practice, to more fully understand why I made the choices that I've made in life, and to understand my clients better. It has made me a much more compassionate social services worker and has also aided me in helping others navigate their own life's journey.

Things to think about:

1. What was the broken pottery in the story?

2. What shattered it?

3. What is the gold filling?

4. What is the lesson and the transformation?

Hope Through Hardship

Joni and Friends

On a hot July afternoon in 1967, Joni Eareckson Tada's life was dramatically altered in a split second. She had just graduated from high school and was ready to attend college to become a physical therapist. Her sister wanted Joni to take a quick swim with her into the Chesapeake Bay, where they lived in Maryland. Joni spotted a raft to dive off into what she thought was deep water.

It wasn't.

That reckless dive into shallow water severed her spinal cord; in other words, it broke her neck. That dive took that athletic seventeen-year-old woman to a life as a quadriplegic in a wheelchair.

Her autobiography and movie, both called *Joni*, describe her journey and struggle with her new physical and emotional state after the accident. Joni plays herself in the movie. She described her bouts with depression and suicidal thoughts that came upon her. [2]

This is also where you can see how she learned to paint with a brush in her mouth, as she is a very talented artist. In a 2003 interview on *Larry King Live*, [3] she shared how when she was first given the paintbrush to put into her mouth by the occupational therapist in the rehab hospital, she would angrily spit it out. The occupational therapist would gently pick up the brush, wipe it off with alcohol, and put it back into Joni's mouth. This went on for some time, with Joni becoming quite angry at the thought of painting with her mouth, until she witnessed the occupational therapist teaching another quadriplegic to write the alphabet with a brush in his mouth. This patient was worse off than Joni was. He was using a ventilator tube to breathe with.

Joni found herself rooting for him to be able to write the alphabet and to be successful. This helped her to realize that there are always those worse off than you are and that when you help others, you can get out of depression because you are no longer focused on yourself.

With this view, in 1979, Joni began to serve the disabled community all over the world through the ministry Joni and Friends, which started quite small. [4] The ministry website describes Joni's many accomplishments, awards, and work

---

[2] https://www.amazon.com/gp/video/detail/amzn1.dv.gti.52b4816b-44f6-6339 a20a -7958174ce390?ref_=imdbref_tt_wbr_pvs_piv&tag=imdbtag_tt_wbr_pvs_piv-20

[3] Larry King Live interview – Jan. 23, 2021, Joni and Friends, https://youtu.be/P_ ItOxB-JpM

[4] "Our History," Joni and Friends, accessed March 15, 2023, joniandfriends.org.

all over the world helping those who are affected by disability. As of today, the Joni and Friends ministry is still going strong and has had a worldwide outreach for more than forty years.

Joni's story is not one of a woman that had a terrible accident and then became a heroine breezing through life encountering fame and fortune.

Far from it.

Joni also deals with more than quadriplegia; she has fought battles against two different cancers and has daily struggles with chronic pain.

However, she often shares on her radio program, interviews, and writings that she also experiences the joys of leading a global outreach to people living with disability. Her story of hope has resonated with millions of disabled people as well as the abled around the world.

Her message is the power of God's love to transform, as well as the triumph of faith over pain and suffering.

What impresses me most about her, aside from all her accomplishments and contributions to the world, is her sweet and humble spirit that always finds the good in whatever trials she has gone through. She has a lovely personality and sincerity that shines through when she shares her heart with others. Joni made a choice to give to others after her accident, and her attitude and her life reflect this.

You can learn more about her at joniandfriends.org.

Things to think about:

1. What was the broken pottery in the story?

2. What shattered it?

3. What is the gold filling?

4. What is the lesson and the transformation?

The Sound of Music

Beethoven

Ludwig van Beethoven, a German composer and pianist, is considered one of the greatest composers of all time. Despite his numerous accomplishments and contributions to classical music, Beethoven faced several adversities in his lifetime, including deafness, poverty, and personal tragedy. Yet he persevered and continued to create timeless masterpieces that have inspired countless musicians and music lovers over the centuries.

His road to success was not without obstacles. When he was a young man, his music teacher, Christian Gottlob Neefe, declared him to be a "hopeless" composer. Despite this initial setback, Beethoven refused to give up on his dream and continued to develop his craft.

He began his musical studies at a young age under the tutelage of Neefe, who was the court organist in Bonn, Germany.

Although Beethoven showed promise as a young musician, Neefe expressed little faith in his abilities as a composer. Despite this criticism, Beethoven was determined to prove his teacher wrong. He spent countless hours practicing and perfecting his craft, eventually producing works that demonstrated his unique vision and creative genius.

Beethoven began to lose his hearing at the age of twenty-six, and by the age of forty-four, he was completely deaf. Despite this setback, Beethoven continued to compose music and remained active as a conductor and performer. He wrote some of his most famous works, including the Ninth Symphony and the late piano sonatas, after he had become completely deaf. This demonstrates Beethoven's determination and resilience in the face of his adversity.

In addition to his hearing loss, Beethoven faced financial difficulties throughout much of his life. He struggled to make ends meet and was often in debt. Despite this, he refused to compromise on his artistic vision and continued to work tirelessly on his compositions.

Beethoven also experienced personal tragedy, including the loss of his mother and several close friends. Despite these difficulties, he remained focused on his work and continued to produce some of his most innovative compositions.

He never gave up and continued to create music that continues to captivate audiences to this day. His perseverance and unwavering commitment to his art are a testament to the human spirit and its ability to overcome even the greatest of challenges.

1. What was the broken pottery in the story?

2. What shattered it?

3. What is the gold filling?

4. What is the lesson and the transformation?

SHILOH ISRAEL CHILDREN'S FUND

Healing Children's Hearts Wracked by Terror

In 2004, David Rubin established the Shiloh Israel Children's Fund in order to help children recover from trauma. The organization offers therapeutic, educational, and recreational programs.

The mission is "to heal the trauma of children who are victims of terror, resulting in a brighter future for the children in the heartland of Israel."

David has shared his story on the fund's website, shilohisraelchildren.org, and it is reprinted here with his permission:

On December 17, 2001, David Rubin and his then 3-year-old son Ruby were driving home from Jerusalem when a hail of terrorists' bullets struck their car.

"The car went totally dead," David recalls. "We were rolling down the road. I turned the ignition, and it didn't start – and they were still shooting! I turned around to look at my 3-year-old, who was sitting in the baby seat behind me, and I noticed that his eyes were open, and he was breathing. He looked like he was trying to cry, but no sounds could come out of his mouth."

With blood gushing from his leg, David realized he was not the only one in the car who was wounded. A bullet from a Kalashnikov assault rifle had cut through the back of Ruby's neck, coming within a millimeter of killing him on the spot.

Miraculously, the car finally started – and David somehow managed to rush himself and his son to a hospital.

David has shared "when I saw all the psychological trauma that my son Ruby was going through, I had this vision of a therapeutic educational campus that would heal the trauma of terror victim children, restore the lost innocence to their lives and, at the same time, rebuild the biblical heartland of Israel. At that moment I decided to start what would eventually become the Shiloh Israel Children's Fund."

After two years of operations, post-trauma therapy, and doctors' visits that healed both him and his son, David began delivering his heartrending testimony to people around the world – spreading the truth about what's really happening in the Land of Israel and encouraging others to give the children of Israel a brighter future.

David strongly believes that, when the world understands the historical and current facts about Shiloh, many will join him in helping the children. This firm belief has given him the strength to overcome his own personal trauma and to turn evil into good in his own life and the lives of others.

The website is shilohisraelchildren.org.

Things to think about:

1. What was the broken pottery in the story?

2. What shattered it?

3. What is the gold filling?

4. What is the lesson and the transformation?

Astrid's Story: How One Happiness Seeker Beat Cancer with Sparkles and Joy

Contributed by Astrid Mueller

with quotes from an interview with Sarah Lapidus

"It all seemed unreal," Astrid Mueller said. She had just recently found a golf-ball sized lump in her breast and was laying still for an ultrasound, and she observed that the nurse was awfully quiet.

Moments later, the nurse left the room, forgetting to shut down the computer screen. There it was, on the ultrasound in front of her: a black mass in her right breast.

"What I saw looked concerning. Somehow, I knew this was probably not good," Mueller said.

Her doctors told her to quickly travel to Anchorage from her home on Kodiak Island to see a breast cancer specialist for more tests.

"I remember that everyone was freaking out around me. I had to take a few breaths to stay calm," Mueller recalled. "One of the first things I did was to speak with my spiritual mentor. I wanted to know if I would be okay."

For Mueller, faith and a higher power helped her immensely.

"It doesn't matter what you believe in. For me, I got the absolute inner certainty that my journey would be a mere blip in my reality and that I would be okay," she said.

"I did find tremendous peace and trust in that, for my whole healing journey," Mueller added.

Mueller remembered she was just entering a health food store in Anchorage when she received the test results. She had stage four breast cancer. She felt surprisingly calm. She was ready for the challenge.

Mueller, a designer and business coach originally from Switzerland, was instantly put on chemotherapy. She was given only one weekend to rush back to Kodiak, pack up her belongings, and move to Anchorage for several months for treatments to save her life. She had a lot of help to pack and relocate from close friends and even her ex-husband.

"So much kindness and support showed up! I'll be forever grateful," Mueller said. "It was insane, just giving up everything that quickly and finding a room to stay in a noisy city I didn't care for, without the friends, the nature, and dogs I was used to." [5]

It was a dark and difficult winter for her. Not only was she in a new place without her community to help her, but the side effects of chemo were difficult to navigate. She felt nauseous and weak, often finding it difficult to even know what to eat.

That wasn't all: when she was diagnosed with cancer, she was also on a business sabbatical, looking for a new direction for her business without a steady income and without any savings.

She put a lot of inner pressure on herself at first. But eventually she realized how unhealthy her inner pressure, worries, and heavy feelings felt. It was as if an inner voice was saying, "If I want to get well, I have to create wellness feelings!" Mueller said.

That was when she decided to choose joy.

"As soon as I decided to do that, I felt like a huge weight was lifted off me," she said. "I get to choose things that would make me happy. Like join that creative class that makes me feel so good. And not always worry about money," Mueller said, adding that it felt like a breath of fresh air.

She didn't take this joy idea lightly but rather with determination. She described it as "a radical act of self-love."

---

[5] This and some other quotes are taken from Sarah Lapidus, "Living Sparkly: How One Palmer Resident Survived Cancer Through Joy," *The People's Paper,* May 2022, https://issuu.com/make-a-scene/docs/the_peoples_paper_may_2022_for_web.

Mueller would ask herself in each moment: "What does my heart want? What will lead me to more joy?" And then she kept taking actions to accomplish those desires.

Her consistent quest for joy didn't just lead her to activities that brought her immediate, fleeting happiness, but rather, it gradually helped her transform her life.

"I became kinder to myself with my inner dialogue. Instead of beating myself up, I focused on what I CAN do. That's also when I started spelling CANcer with capitalized first three letters," Mueller said, laughing.

She also had to make some tough decisions, like letting some people and some things go.

 "I had to learn to trust myself, over anyone or anything else. That was super scary at first, but it ended up being a huge blessing eventually. I found so much strength," she said.

Her focus on joy soon also helped her in treatments.

The clinic she visited for treatments seemed drab, with "puke-colored" walls, harsh fluorescent lighting, no music, and hardly any plants.

Mueller recalled that her senses were hypersensitive from the medications, and things that may seem insignificant to others (like hearing the clicking sound of chemotherapy machines) were amplified in the emotional impact they created for her.

The clinic surroundings made her feel sick and unhappy.

"This was a blessing in disguise for me because I became hyper-aware of how important joy actually is for our health. Also, when it comes to our environment," she said.

Mueller began to speak up more as well and asking for what she wanted.

"It wasn't about being demanding; it was about saying yes to me and my wellness. You can ask for things kindly," she said.

Whenever she noticed something would help her feel better, she asked for it. Like asking someone to remove an open trash can with visible syringes because it made her feel queasy.

When requests weren't possible, she got creative on her own terms. She regularly brought two heavy bags of feel-good items to chemo sessions. She also decided to dress up sparkly. Armed with her headphones, she chose positive and healing music and sounds. She also brought a lamp with her for better lighting, her own plant, colors and crayons, and inspiring cards and books. She even rearranged furniture.

"They had chairs facing corners! Can you believe it?" Mueller said. As a designer, she was shocked and took charge by turning her chair to the window for a blue-sky view.

"Creative thinking always helps! And if you can't do anything at a moment, you can stay curious, trust things will be okay, and in the meantime, change the way you look at things," Mueller said. "Certain thoughts will create joy. Others can create anxiety. I didn't like to use the word *chemo's* for instance, so I called them 'healing elixirs.' That definitely felt better."

Mueller used her coaching experience to become her own biggest advocate for wellness. More than ever, she realized that health wasn't just about the physical body but also overall wellness. This includes emotions, and the happiness of the soul and the mind, she said. As one of her wellness mindset techniques, she started using reframing techniques to feel more empowered.

"When I didn't like how something was worded, I chose my own words. I even used a reframe for my whole healing journey. Instead of looking at cancer like something terrible that I had to go through, I chose to see it as a 'spa cleansing into love.' That not only felt better, but it made me feel strong. Everything felt very purposeful with my own new way of looking at it. We can do so much with our thoughts!" she said excitedly.

The more Mueller focused on self-love, joy, and thoughts and actions that brought her happiness, the more she realized that she could make it through even the hardest of challenges. She referred to this lifestyle as "living with sparkle."

"Gradually, I was able to turn my whole healing journey into an empowering experience, feeling mostly calm, discovering huge inner resilience," she remembered.

Her joy and "sparkle" were infectious and spread to the staff and patients around her.

"When we sparkle from the inside out, it's contagious. All we have to do is give ourselves permission to sparkle," she said, like her book *Permission To Sparkle*.

Her positive mindset and actions positively impacted her healing: After her last set of treatments, her doctor was stunned, saying that Mueller's bloodwork kept improving even during her most potent chemo sessions.

In her doctor's experience, for most patients, lab results tended to worsen during the harsher treatment sessions. Not for Mueller: in the words of her oncology doctor Dr. Kendal Webb, she "walked away with the blood of a healthy person!"

Mueller said it wasn't always easy. One big "whammy" happened to her when in the summer of 2021, one of her oncology doctors used the unfortunate wording of "Do you know what stage of cancer you have? You have stage four. That cannot be healed."

That was one of the moments where her joy focus and mindset was especially put to the test.

"I was shaken at first, but I stood my ground," she recalled. "I told my doctor, 'This will not be my reality. I will walk away from this healed. I need you to also believe this with me. Can you do this?' "

An open and mutually beneficial conversation ensued, where Mueller got to learn more about her doctor's "superpowers," such as geeking out about the latest medical oncology technologies, and that he also had the best intentions for her, but that as a doctor, he was not able to use words like "cured" or "healed," Mueller said, assuming this was for legal reasons.

The conversation ended in a better mutual understanding and with her doctor agreeing, "Yes. If anyone could, I could walk out of this hospital without any cancer evident," Mueller said.

After a rather long healing journey with chemotherapies, surgeries, and radiation, as well as holistic healing methods like energy healing, spiritual mentoring, creativity, acupuncture, and nutrition, Mueller received her clean bill of health in October 2022, with no disease evident.

Since going through cancer, Mueller says she discovered a deeper sense of purpose in her work to share what she has learned, to inspire others to create their own "joy sparkle lives," and to also "THRIVE through CANcer, and for life!"

Today, Astrid Mueller lives in the beautiful quaint town of Palmer, Alaska, surrounded by pretty mountains, a kind community, and doggie love, and she supports CANcer patients around the world.

Mueller is a published author, designer, brand consultant, and now also CANcer wellness consultant to patients and clinics. Astrid Mueller can be reached at www.AstridMueller.com

Things to think about:

1. What was the broken pottery in the story?

2. What shattered it?

3. What is the gold filling?

4. What is the lesson and the transformation?

MAN'S SEARCH FOR MEANING

Viktor Frankl

Viktor Frankl was an Austrian neurologist and psychologist who lived through one of the most traumatic experiences of human history: the Holocaust. He faced extreme adversity but emerged from this experience with a profound understanding of the human condition and a desire to help others find meaning in their own lives. Through his work as a therapist and his writing, he became one of the most influential thinkers of the twentieth century, helping countless people find meaning and purpose in the face of their own challenges.

He was born in Vienna in 1905 and grew up in a middle-class family. He studied medicine and became a practicing neurologist and psychiatrist, but his life changed dramatically when the Nazis came to power in Austria in 1938. Frankl was arrested and sent to a concentration camp, where he endured years of physical and emotional abuse. Despite the brutal conditions, he refused to lose hope or give up his sense of purpose. Instead, he used his experience to develop a new theory of psychology that he called *logotherapy.*

Frankl's logotherapy was based on the idea that human beings are driven for a search for meaning, and that this search is what gives life its purpose. He argued that the key to finding the meaning of life is to identify one's unique "mission" or "vocation" and to pursue it with all one's heart and soul. This idea was revolutionary in the field of psychology, and it resonated deeply with people who were struggling to find meaning in their own lives.

His writing and teaching has a profound impact on people all over the world, especially in the aftermath of World War II. He wrote several books, including the classic *Man's Search for Meaning,* which became a bestseller and has been translated into dozens of languages.

Through his work, Frankl inspired people to find meaning in their own lives, even in the face of adversity. He showed people that it is possible to overcome the greatest challenges and find joy, fulfillment, and purpose, no matter what life throws their way.

Everything can be taken from a man but one thing: the last of the human freedoms—to choose one's attitude in any given set of circumstances, to choose one's own way.

When we are no longer able to change a situation, we are challenged to change ourselves.

*- **Viktor Frankl,** from* Man's Search for Meaning [6]

---

[6] Viktor Frankl, *Man's Search for Meaning* (Boston: Beacon Press, 2006), 112

Things to think about:

1. What was the broken pottery in the story?

2. What shattered it?

3. What is the gold filling?

4. What is the lesson and the transformation?

SLOW LEARNERS, SOBRIETY, SELF-FORGIVENESS, AND PERSONAL PEACE

By Doug F. in Alaska

We all have our individual stories of how we got into AA, our journey once there, and where it has taken us in our lives. Some of us hit our bottom hard, came to AA as totally defeated souls, and if we "kept coming back" and worked the steps, have evolved to a sober and happy life without so-called relapses. Others of us, "slow learners" like myself, took many years in and out of the program and therefore in and out of sobriety before that happened.

My story isn't unique or unusual. There wasn't much drinking in my immediate family. My folks might have a "high ball" or glass of wine at a holiday meal, but that was it. I was an only child in a loving middle-class home and just never thought about drinking alcohol one way or another growing up. While some thought of me as a "straight arrow" in high school in the early 1950s, I was never aware of much drinking by my classmates in that era.

That all changed when I went away to college to study engineering. I joined a fraternity, and weekend parties became the norm where mostly beer was served. The 3.2% form of the beverage was then legal for eighteen-year-olds in Ohio. Because of our tough engineering curriculum, very little partying was done during the week, but on the weekends, look out! As a rather geeky young man, I found I loved the feeling I got after a few beers. As I have heard it said many times later in AA, it made me "comfortable in my own skin."

I looked forward to those weekends, but I managed to get homework, lab reports, etc. done over the weekend and it didn't seem to affect me. Now looking back, I realize it gave me an exaggerated sense of my social skills, especially with the opposite sex! It also turned out that even then I had a common alcoholic characteristic. I could consume a lot of alcohol before it affected me on the outside. I didn't look or act drunk. On the occasional weekend hangovers that I would have, I now realize I actually bordered on alcohol poisoning before I could stop. At the time, it was one of those routine events that just happened when you had too much to drink.

In spite of all this, I made it through college and got a job in another state with a large international company in one of their engineering departments. I was engaged to a girl I met in college. We soon got married and seemed to be settling down to a "normal" middle class life. I would routinely have a couple of beers in the evening, but drinking wasn't a major issue. However, as life went on and kids were born, work pressures and overtime increased along with business trips thrown into the mix, the evening drinking became more important, especially when I was out of town and didn't have to be home by a reasonable time or otherwise be accountable.

Poor judgment, and the resulting inappropriate behavior, started occurring during these "travel binges" with the usual hangovers and guilt feelings the following day. Meanwhile, during regular workdays, occasional stopping for "a couple of brews" at a bar after work became more frequent and started a pattern of getting home later and later with the lying involved and the marital distress that created.

Finally, I decided to stop drinking altogether. I managed to stop for almost a year, but I always felt "strung out." One day my wife and I had an argument about something, I don't even recall what it was about, and I stormed out of the house. I then went on a two-day drunken binge before I came home, destroying any trust I had built up over the year.

This pattern continued for a year or more when I finally agreed to get some counseling after one binge after which I seriously considered suicide. Today I realize my counselor was clueless about alcoholism and wanted to probe my background, Sigmund Freud style, when all I wanted to know was, "Why do I drink?" After giving up on me, he did say, "Well, you might try AA. It works for some people!" So I got my first start in AA.

I eventually joined a group in our small town and got a sponsor. He and I talked about the steps, but I never really did them. I stayed sober for almost five years even during a family tragedy. Although I called myself an alcoholic at meetings, it wasn't heartfelt. I still felt guilty about the things I had done when I was drinking, but as long as life was going at an even keel, I chose to ignore those feelings. The damage done to the marriage never was addressed, and finally we separated. Following a now established pattern, I went out again. A good AA friend eventually confronted me and got me back into the rooms of AA.

I won't go into the next ten years in detail, but I unwisely got remarried to a much younger woman, moved to another state, and eventually got divorced again. Each time I had a life crisis, I went back to secretly drinking, then back to AA. I can say now that AA did at least save my life, but with seventeen years of intermittent sobriety!

Finally, as my second marriage started to fail and after going out again, I decided enough was enough. Obviously, my way had never worked. I had been around AA long enough to know what I really needed to do. I signed into an outpatient program that was great and I learned a lot of new information, but the real difference was this time *I made a decision to become willing.* I finally made an admission down deep in my gut that "I am truly an alcoholic" and was willing to do what others have done to stay sober, joyous, and free.

A few months after completing outpatient, I went to an annual AA weekend retreat in our area that featured fourth and fifth step sessions. [See the end of Doug's story for details on these steps.] I had never, even in the outpatient program, done a sincere and meaningful fourth step. For the first time in the solitude of the little private rooms we had at the retreat, I really tried to write all my fears and events for which I felt guilty exactly as it tells you in the Big Book. I then signed up for doing a fifth step with this new brutally honest information. I did this fifth step with a former Catholic priest who had some similar experiences and now was sober and happily married with kids!

After hearing my finally honest and emotional fourth step, he sensed immediately that I had been beating myself up with guilt for all the turmoil and stress I had put on my wives and children through my drinking. For the first time in my life, I had the humility to join him as we both got on our knees and he prayed, saying, "God, help this man forgive himself for the things he has done in his former life and help to give him a new one." We did the sixth and seventh step afterwards, although this was somewhat of a blur. I went back to my little room and sat quietly and then took a short nap. When I awoke, I strangely felt different and calm. *I can honestly say I had a spiritual experience.* I ultimately asked this man to be my sponsor. He was willing and I was willing. He helped me through my second divorce sober and doing it in the best interests of all.

Since that afternoon at this life changing AA retreat, I have not had a single instance of a desire to drink, and I have found a peace and a new happiness that is talked about in the Big Book. The person I am today can look back on that man that I was and feel compassion for him instead of guilt. In retirement, for the right reasons this time, I found the love of my life with whom I share this new existence. We recently moved to a new state to be near her children and grandchildren and are enjoying the adventure. I make sure I have a home group that I regularly attend wherever I live and do service work when I can. This spring I will be picking up a nineteen–year medallion. As an old AA friend with long-term sobriety where I used to live often said, "Today I am at peace with God, the world, my family, and my neighbors, most of the time!"

Note from Hillary:

As told in the "Big Book" of Alcoholics Anonymous (AA), the fourth step is to make "a searching and fearless moral inventory of ourselves." This step involves taking a deep and honest look at oneself, identifying character defects, and facing personal shortcomings.

The fifth step of AA is to admit "to God, to ourselves, and to another human being the exact nature of our wrongs." This step involves sharing the inventory made in the previous step with a trusted friend, sponsor, or spiritual advisor. The goal of this step is to take responsibility for one's actions, make amends where possible, and move forward with a renewed sense of purpose and direction.

The sixth step is to become "entirely ready to have God remove all these defects of character." This step involves a willingness to let go of negative behaviors, thoughts, and attitudes that were identified in the previous step. It requires a commitment to personal growth and a belief that change is possible.

The seventh step of AA is to "humbly [ask] Him to remove our shortcomings." This step involves asking a higher power (as each individual understands it) to remove the negative traits and behaviors that were identified in the previous steps. It requires a willingness to surrender control and trust in the process of spiritual growth.

Overall, the sixth and seventh steps are focused on acknowledging personal faults, preparing to let go of them, and seeking spiritual guidance to overcome them. These steps are seen as critical for achieving long–term sobriety and personal growth. [7]

---

[7] This information is from the "Big Book" of Alcoholics Anonymous and can be found online at https://www.aa.org/twelve-steps-twelve-traditions.

1. What was the broken pottery in the story?

2. What shattered it?

3. What is the gold filling?

4. What is the lesson and the transformation?

FROM BONDAGE TO FREEDOM

Frederick Douglass

Frederick Douglass faced numerous adversities in his life, including slavery, poverty, and limited access to education. He was born into slavery in 1818 in Maryland and was separated from his family at a young age. He was subjected to physical abuse and harsh working conditions as a slave. Despite these challenges, he taught himself to read and write, which was illegal for slaves at the time.

After several failed escape attempts, Douglass finally succeeded in escaping slavery in 1838 and settled in the North as a free man. Although he faced racism and discrimination, he became a prominent abolitionist, speaker, and writer, using his own story to educate and inspire others to fight against slavery. He wrote two influential autobiographies, *Narrative of the Life of Frederick Douglass, an American Slave* and *My Bondage and My Freedom,* which detailed his experiences as a slave and his journey to freedom.

He became such a renowned proponent of abolition that he served as one of President Lincoln's advisors. He was even nominated for vice president in 1872.

Through his speeches, writings, and activism, Douglass played a crucial role in the abolitionist movement and helped to bring attention to the horrors of slavery. He continued to fight for equal rights and against discrimination throughout his life, becoming one of the most prominent figures of the nineteenth century.

Things to think about:

1. What was the broken pottery in the story?

2. What shattered it?

3. What is the gold filling?

4. What is the lesson and the transformation?

FREEDOM HOUSE – THE STORY OF FOUNDER JENNIFER WALLER

Part 1

Journey to Freedom

I interviewed Jennifer several months ago after listening to her radio show while I was driving in the Mat-Su Valley of Alaska. Her story has been lightly edited for clarity.

...

I was born and raised right here in Sterling, Alaska. I was raised in the church my whole life as well, but we lost a sister in a three-wheeler accident. She passed away when I was about six years old, and it really was devastating. There were six of us kids in our family, and my mom ended up taking that very hard.

She drank to numb herself. So, at about six years old, even though we went to church every Sunday, things became rocky at home, and long story short, I grew up saying I'd never drink or do drugs. I'm a middle child, and I did really well in school, as I was in varsity soccer and varsity cheerleading, and I loved life. In about tenth grade, I tried marijuana for the first time. This was an absolute gateway drug in my life because I then started drinking on the weekends, and then I started dating this guy that was selling marijuana. He was like a dealer, and at that time, it wasn't legal, and it just started with partying on the weekends. I graduated high school at the top of the class, 4.0, and I had started college locally at Kenai Peninsula College. I was going to be a nurse, and I had a whole outlook planned. My boyfriend went from selling marijuana to harder drugs, such as cocaine and oxycontin pills, and I just kind of went along with whatever was in the house and whatever was next.

We had a daughter soon after, and when she was about two months old, I ended up smoking oxycontin for the first time, and that first time I smoked it, I loved it. It's a manmade heroin, so that's an opiate, and the streets were drenched with it back then. This was about fifteen years ago. One pill of oxycontin was selling for $140. I ended up dropping out of college, fully addicted to this heroin-type substance. My mom and sister were raising our daughter, and I was just living that lifestyle for a while. My boyfriend ended up being very abusive, so he would get arrested for beating on me, and then as soon as he'd get out of jail, I'd go pick him up, and it was just this vicious cycle of darkness.

At this time, in 2004, my dad approached me. He's never had an addiction problem. He's been just such an anchor, the pillar in our family, and said, "You need help." I was twenty-one years old. He said, "I found this rehab in Phoenix, Arizona. Will you go? I also found that you've been stealing from me and forging my checks for your drug addiction, so if you don't go, I'm going to turn you in to the cops."

So, at twenty-one, I chose rehab. Actually, it was me and my mom, because at that same time, my dad approached my mom and said, "You need help. Will you go to this?" She was addicted to substances also. So, my mom and I flew out together and attended my first inpatient rehab, thirty days there in a treatment center. Then from there, I moved to Ohio because I didn't want to come back to Sterling, where it was just too much darkness, and everyone I knew was making the wrong choices.

So, I moved to Ohio, where my grandparents lived, and that's where I met who is now my husband, working at a factory there. He had a son, I had a daughter, and then we got married just nine months after meeting. I ended up fully back in my addiction within a couple months because down in Ohio, the same pill that was going for $140 here in Alaska was $40 on the streets there and there was an abundance of them. I ended up relapsing back into my addiction for about a year. I was so sick and tired of being sick and tired. I couldn't even function, and I was mixing alcohol with pills, and I lost jobs and couldn't be a mom.

I said to my husband, "I need to move back to Alaska." I just told him "I'm going back to Alaska." My husband is not an addict. He's never done drugs in his life. He was working full time, trying to raise our kids, trying to keep me alive. He said, "Well, give me two weeks. I'm going to sell everything." That's where he was born and raised, in Ohio. So we sold everything and drove up in 2006, back to Alaska, and what I was doing—not knowing it at the time—was running from myself. But no matter where I ran, there I was.

So, we moved all the way back across the country to Alaska. Here I am thinking, "Okay, now I've got all my family around me. I can get help again," but all my using people were still using, there at the same spots, with the same dealers, so my addiction continued for another year and a half, and in that time, we got pregnant with our first child together. By the grace of God, even throughout my addiction, I delivered an eight-and-a-half-pound baby boy. God just had to have protected him that whole time because even while I was pregnant with him, I was breaking in and robbing businesses. I was stealing to support my habit. I was stealing from my husband's work. I mean, I was just an absolute mess.

My baby was about nine months old when I had overdosed for something like the fifth time, and I would end up in the hospital and be hooked up to heart monitors for months at a time because I was really messing up my heart, mixing all these drugs and alcohol. I ended up going back to a rehab here locally, called Serenity House in Soldotna. I did thirty-three days inpatient there, and then I graduated, and for the first time in almost eight years at that point, I got nine months clean and sober. I was working the steps, working the program, and also going to church because my older sister had invited me back. I had walked away from God for eight years at this point. You know, I was raised in the church, but I had all the head knowledge of who He was and all the Bible songs and verses, but I did not have a relationship with Jesus.

So I went back to this rehab and graduated. My husband's super proud of me. I'm trying, trying, trying. But there were these secrets that we talk about in recovery. There's a saying, "You're only as sick as your secrets," and there was this stuff I wasn't willing to admit, these sins that I had committed that led me to thinking, "I don't want anyone to know. I'm not going to make amends for those. I'll do this, this, and this, but not this," and man, I just kept stuffing that, stuffing that, and what God was trying to do was to get me to ask forgiveness so that He could work through it and heal me through it, but instead of working through it, I ended up drinking again. And within six hours of that first drink, after nine months, I was looking for heroin and pills and went back into a full relapse for almost three months.

My husband and I had filled out divorce paperwork. He was going to take the kids and move back to Ohio, where he's from, because I was again, on my face, robbing people; I wouldn't come home for days, just a mess. So, we had filled out the divorce paperwork, and then I was again in an overdose state, and the people I was with dropped me off at my oldest sister's house, and I couldn't even stand. I was dry heaving. I was puking. She scooped me up, took me back to the hospital, and that's our local rehab, which is run through our hospital. They saw it was a drug addiction issue, so the director of the rehab came in and said, "Can you have your bags packed and ready for rehab in the morning at 10?"

I was just so hopeless because I'd already been to two rehabs. This would be my third rehab. I'd tried psychiatrists. I'd tried medicine. I'd tried everything that I could think of, and here I was, almost dead again in the hospital, and my husband was leaving me, and my kids were leaving me, and I had just destroyed every relationship around me. I did say, "Yes, I'll be there," but that morning, when my husband did drop me off at the rehab center, I took a handful of pills and chased it with whiskey in the bathroom because I didn't want to live anymore. That day, on June 25, 2009, I tried to take my life because I was believing the enemy's voice, that I'll always be this way, I'll never change, this is who I'll always be, and my husband and kids are leaving, so I've nothing else to live for.

Thankfully, by the grace of God, three days later—because I had been in a blackout state for three days—I woke up on June 28, 2009, in that rehab again, and I remember opening my eyes, and it was like, "Oh man, I'm here again." But then at the same moment, it was this verse that I had learned as a little girl, at a VBS camp, that God used. I learned it as a song, but it's Psalm 119:105, and it says, "Thy word is a lamp unto my feet, and a light unto my path,"[8] and that's the verse He used that just started running through my head, and I just started singing that song, and I started weeping, and I got up that morning. It was six in the morning. I'll never forget this. I had a roommate. She rolled over and she said, "What are you doing?" I hit my knees, and I raised my arms, and I just surrendered my life and my will and everything to Jesus, and I said, "I can't do this. I don't want to live, but I know You can in me and through me."

So, June 26, 2009, is my sobriety birthday, but June 28, 2009, is the day that I entered into relationship with my King of Kings, and all I had was a pile of broken ashes. I said, "Lord, here. Here's what I have." And that's all He needed. He just breathed into that pile of ashes, and restored and healed, of course, over time. I've celebrated thirteen years clean and sober this year. When I got out of that rehab, my husband was supposed to have gone to Ohio. Well, he ended up staying, and through a year of counseling and prayer—we went and saw our pastor once a month—God just restored our marriage. We'll celebrate seventeen years of marriage this January. We now have four kids. He had one, I had one, and now we've had two together. And I get to be their mom, and I got to raise them for the last thirteen years.

---

[8] Scripture quotations are taken from the King James Version (public domain).

Part 2

Freedom House

My oldest daughter was seven when I got sober, my son was two, and then our youngest daughter was born when I was still addicted and using. God has redeemed and restored that family unit, what the devil had almost completely demolished. From that, out of the five of us siblings that were left, because we had lost a sister, four of us ended up in addictions, four out of five of us kids. I have a sister that has been arrested more than thirty-five times. What was happening is I was going into our local prison and visiting her, bringing her devotions in, trying to speak life into her, and she gave me an idea. She said, "Why don't you sign up for prison ministry? Because they come in and do Bible studies here with all the girls in prison." So, I did that for a year and a half into my sobriety. I became a prison volunteer.

But when God saved me, He put that fire in me to not only share my story, but to reach back into the pit of hell around me . . .

Being in the state of Alaska, we're number one in everything bad—addiction, suicide, domestic violence, alcohol addiction— so I ended up going to nine different villages with different groups and doing outreach missions and sharing my story, and also working through our local prison. We're just pretrial for women, so I approached the state chaplain up in Anchorage because they have chaplains paid for the men, but our women had nothing, and they couldn't get a Bible. They had nothing going on.

I went up to Anchorage, had this meeting, and said, "We really need to get some teachings and some Bibles and some discipleship in there," and he said, "Well, perfect. How about you?"

So I became the female chaplain down here at our local Wildwood Prison. I did that for about a year and a half, and that's when God laid this on my heart because these women were doing amazing. They would come to Bible studies. They would be taking notes. They'd get released, and there they'd come back again, another thirty days later, the same ladies. I'd ask, "What happened? Why are you back?"

It was the same story all over again. They'd say, "When I got released, I had to go to the same place that I came from, which was toxic, and there's drugs, and it's abusive, or I would be homeless on the streets in Alaska." It was in February when this girl came up to me at a Bible study in prison, and she said, "Jenny, do you know of anywhere I can go? I get out at 7:00 in the morning." It was 20 below zero. She said, "If I go back to where I came from, I'm going to die. I know it." I had to look at her and tell her, "There's nowhere for you to go here. We have no . . . There's no room in the inn," and her eyes filled with tears, and she said, "I'll sleep in the basement of a church. Anywhere. Please, I want to live. I want to live."

I went home that night, and I was weeping in my prayer closet with the Lord, and I thought, "I don't even want to go back in there because this is too hard for me to see the pain and send them back to where they came from."

It was that day that I wrote in my prayer journal, "I want you to open a home for women." That's what the Spirit spoke to me.

I just closed it up, and I just prayed on it for months and months, and about three months later, I felt that just as strong, so I went and I spoke with five pastors in our local area that had been mentoring me, that knew me, that had been helping me. At this point, I'm seven years sober. I do rehab ministry, prison ministry, street ministry, full time, never was working. My husband, thankfully, was able to support us.

I went to these five pastors, and said, "This is my vision. What do you think?" All five said, "Yes. Do it. We're behind you." So long story short, I Googled how to form a nonprofit. I had never been on a board, I don't know anything about a board of directors, but one of my favorite sayings is, "With God and Google, you can do almost anything."

Basically, what I did was I called people that were doing prison ministry with me because I knew they had the same heart, they had the same passions. They were Spirit-filled and Spirit-led, so I just asked my friends, "Will you be on this board? This is my vision," and we formed our board, had our first board meeting, of "what is this going to look like?" And then we started looking for homes in the area.

Long story short, where I'm sitting is our women's house. It's 5,000 square feet, but the building itself was about $250,000, and the city inspector came over and said I had to do about a half a million dollars in renovations in order to open. We're right in the heart of Soldotna because it's so important. Ninety percent of our residents come with no driver's license or no vehicle. So, I knew for success, they'd have to be able to get to meetings, to treatment, to groups, to doctors' appointments, to jobs, to residences, to the grocery store because we don't have a vehicle, and they didn't. This spot was perfect, but it was going to be three quarters of a million dollars to purchase and renovate.

I talked with the owner of the building. She was able to cosign for us because we're a two-month-old nonprofit. The bank isn't going to give us a mortgage loan. We're in an escrow with her, and then I just started going to these churches that invited me and allowed me in to cast the vision and share my heart and get volunteers to come and work.

We signed the paperwork December 17, 2016, and the city inspector came to us. He walked through for four hours, wrote everything, a half a million dollars, and he kept asking me, "Where are you going to get the money?" Because I had told him we're not getting any grants, no insurance, because we're going to be Jesus Christ–centered. The power of forgiveness and the power of the living God is going to do this. We're going to disciple, and we're going to teach women, at the time, what the Bible says.

His words to me were, "I don't believe in the same God that you do, but what you're trying to do here is impossible." And he had written on our permit it's going to take us three to five years for the demolition of the building to make it compliant with ADA, the Americans with Disabilities Act, and it will take three to five years pending funding is what it said.

Four months later, that same city inspector stood in our kitchen with tears coming down his face, handing me the permit of occupancy because God completed a half a million dollars in renovations in four months. Completely paid for. With just public donations.

Not a single grant, not a single borough, state, nothing. It was all the churches that would do love offerings. I would go speak somewhere, and God told me in the beginning to never ask for money. So anytime I ever spoke, or was invited, I never even mentioned the word *money*, and they would take like a love offering, and I'd get $8,000 here, and then I'd get $10,000 here. We had a volunteer log. Every time anyone came on the property, for insurance, they had to sign in, sign out. We had more than five hundred people donate more than 2,500 labor hours, so all the actual labor was donated by community members, men's groups, and youth groups, and everybody got to swing a hammer, and we had to tear out walls and staircases. It was a huge, huge project, but God completed it in just four months, and we welcomed our very first resident May 1, 2017.

We've been open here for six years now at the women's house, and again, our operating budget was about ten grand a month. We're completely donation driven to this day. We still don't get any grants because we won't compromise. We have devotions twice a week in the morning, we have Bible study once a week, and we have chapels the first Tuesday of every month. Those are all required if you live here. A company once said, "We'll give you this $50,000 if you make it optional." That's all we would have to do is change the word from *required* to *optional*, "and you'll get fifty grand." It was like the enemy just dangling this little carrot, but I said, "Nope. Thank you so much, but we're going to pass."

In the very first year we were open at the women's house, twelve months, we had twenty-three women come in and out. We have nine beds here at the women's house. They can live with us up to a year max, but the average stay is about five months. Whatever they need to successfully transition is our whole goal, whatever that looks like, but we've seen forty-two kids in one year reunited with their mothers out of OCS and state care systems, and that's in one year, and we've been open now six years.

This lady that moved in as a resident, she stayed with us a year. Then we transitioned her into staff, because we have a staff that lives on site full time, so now she's a live-in staff. Well, her daughter just moved in recently, so we have the mom, we have the daughter. Well, the daughter just had a baby. So right now, we have three generations living here at Freedom House, and we are watching the generational curse be broken, and it just makes my heart explode.

About two years in, though, to this being open, it was just me as staff at first. I was the only staff, and I had a couple of volunteers. Two years into being open, we were having men overdosing and suicide and death after death after death. The troopers reached out one day; they have free rein into our homes. We work with the parole officers, the troopers, and OCS very closely. We're highly respected in the area because accountability is one of our three pillars of the ministry. We have accountability, hope, and community. That's our main focus, so we have random drug testing. We do random breathalyzers. We have cameras. We have curfews.

The court system loves us. They just told me recently, "I will only release people to the Freedom Houses," because of our accountability, because we're not playing games, and because we're serious about what we do. We're going to help whoever wants help, but we're not going to let anyone mooch around and sleep all day. They've got to be up and out of their beds at a certain time. Their beds must be made. We've got a strict program.

So, two years into it, I went to my board of directors, and said, "We've got to open a men's home. There are men dying on the streets. I have men in prison that want a safe place," and God showed me at that time that God created man to be the leaders of the homes and of the families, providers, protectors, and spiritual leaders, and just how important it is. If we can get these men discipled and healed and on fire, God's going to heal whole family units.

We had no money. We were paying $10,000 a month to keep the women's house going, and my board, at first, said, "No. We can't." I said, "Well, will you guys just take two weeks and let's pray on it, and let's come back?" So we did that, we came back, and we voted. It was 100 percent yes, that now was the time. I'm so thankful because my board of directors saw the need. I'm a real go-getter, and I'll see something, and think, "Yeah, let's run," and then my board is so amazing because they keep me really balanced and focused, yet allow me to move in the Spirit, which is critical because we literally rely on the Holy Spirit every day—to not only pay the bills, but to give us wisdom on intakes. I have to do dismissals all the time, and if they relapse, we have a zero-tolerance policy for that. However, they can reapply after fifteen days if they've been kicked out for any of our dismissals.

The board said, "Yes, let's pursue this," so I found a building about a mile away. It was $250,000 for the building. I called the city inspector. We only have one. We're a small town. He said, "Let me guess."

This is the same inspector that witnessed the miracle of the women's house. He said, "I heard you want to open a men's house." Then he continued to say, "Well, let me guess. You don't have any money." And I said, "Yes. You're right. Not only do we not have money now, we're going ten grand out every thirty days to run the women's house."

He met me over there. It needed $300,000 in renovations before we could open.

I started casting the vision at churches again. We have just some amazing, amazing churches. I have been able to stand behind seventeen different pulpits to cast the vision to do this, from Homer, Nikiski, Soldotna, Moose Pass, Seward, Sterling, and then a few in Anchorage that I have family members at. We just started volunteering again, and in just twelve weeks this time, God completed $300,000 in renovations, and we opened the men's house in March of 2019. We have twelve beds over there. The need for men is much higher than for women, so we're usually always full at the men's house. Right now, we have the biggest waiting list we've had. We have about sixteen men on our waiting list, waiting to come in.

We've been open three years over there now, and now our budget is $23,000 every thirty days, and by the grace of God and miracles, bills get paid. There are days I don't know how they're going to get paid, and I'll get a knock on the door. This literally happened. I was writing the last amount of a check out, asking God, "I know you didn't open these homes just to close us because we've got to pay heat, mortgages, and we've got a lot of payments." I then got a knock on my door at the office, and it was a young man. I opened it. He said, "My grandma wanted me to drop this envelope off for you," and left, and it was a check for $10,000. I thought, "Of course she did." I was able to pay our bills for that month, and that's literally how many of our bills are paid.

I have story after story. We got a box in the mail a couple of years ago, and it sat on the desk for three days because we now have nine staff and twenty-four volunteers that run the ministry. We've grown, obviously, a ton. I have twenty-one residents between both houses. Our main focus is discipleship, but I was busy. I'm running to and fro, and my other staff member said to me, "Don't forget there's a box on the desk that came in the mail." I said, "Oh, that's right." So I go, and I open it, three days later, dumped out this little box, and there are stacks of twenties. Cash from a little church in Indiana who had heard about us, and the Lord put it on their hearts to take up a love offering, and they sent cash, $10,000 cash, in the mail to us. I mean, I just love how God works, and literally, He pays our bills by faith.

We just keep putting the next foot in front of the other; these are His houses anyway. This is His ministry. These are His sons and daughters, and so He's taught me over the years to trust, to take leaps of faith, to allow Him to get all the glory, and His name be glorified in all of this, and that He's going to provide.

We're chugging right along now, and people from all over the state have lived with us. We've flown people in from Colorado, Oregon, and Washington to live with us. Anyone's eligible. You don't need a referral, but we're not an inpatient treatment center, and we're not a homeless shelter. That's how I like to explain it. We're a long-term recovery residence with a focus on discipleship.

***

At this point in our interview, Jennifer paused, then I asked her, "Is your nickname Nehemiah?"

She replied, "No, but I did that Bible study right when this was all happening, and it was so cool. I've just seen so many similarities."

I then asked her what happened to that woman, the first woman in the prison who said, "I have to find a place; I'm getting out at 7. I can't go back, or I'll die." "Do you know what happened?"

Jennifer replied, "Yes. She's lived with us. She lived with us the first time, ended up going out, making some bad choices. Came back the second time, and right now, she's clean and sober, living on her own."

I asked about her husband, who showed such caring and love for Jennifer through her using years. She replied, "He gave me a taste of forgiveness because when I came out of that rehab that last time, he has never held my past against me. He's only cheered me on for health. He's never brought anything up. And we're talking four-and-a-half years of our marriage at first, it was all darkness. He's shown unconditional love. He would say that he wasn't a Christian when I met him. He had head knowledge of it but didn't give his heart really to God until around the time I was getting sober. I was the one who was pushing for divorce when I was using."

"We had filled out the paperwork. All I had to do was take the paperwork to the courthouse, and I was the one pushing for it, because I hated myself so much, and the enemy was just telling me, 'They'd be better without you,' and I had done a lot of stuff to break trust in the marriage, so I hated myself, and thankfully, I'm not that person. I can tell this story confidently because I am a new creation."

"The old is gone, the new has come, and I look at myself in the mirror, and I like the woman looking back at me."

For more information on Freedom House,

visit https://freedomhouse907.com

Things to think about:

1. What was the broken pottery in the story?

2. What shattered it?

3. What is the gold filling?

4. What is the lesson and the transformation?

If You Don't Get a Miracle, Become One

Nick Vujicic

Nick Vujicic is an Australian motivational speaker, evangelist, and best-selling author who was born on December 4, 1982, with a rare condition known as tetra-amelia syndrome, which caused him to be born without arms or legs. Despite his physical limitations, Nick has become a source of inspiration and motivation to millions of people around the world through his speeches, books, and videos.

I viewed Nick Vujicic being interviewed in a *60 Minutes Australia* interview and an interview with Joni Eareckson Tada on YouTube, [9] and read the content on Nick Vujicic's website, including several articles about him.

---

[9] "S1E0: Joni Eareckson Tada, Nick Vujicic, and Katherine Wolf on What Determines a Person's Value," Joni and Friends channel, YouTube, posted June 29, 2019, https://youtu.be/s_P1I9gx4Jg.

Nick had been bullied in school and had become very depressed. Nick shares in his music video "Something More" that as a ten-year-old child, he tried to commit suicide. [10] At the end of the video, he shares, "If you don't get a miracle... become one."

He refused to let his physical limitations define him, and instead, he chose to focus on his strengths and abilities. Through hard work and determination, Nick learned to do many things that most people take for granted, such as writing, swimming, and even playing the piano with his feet. Though born without arms or legs, he has two small feet, one of which has two toes. The small foot on his left hip helps him balance and enables him to kick. He uses his one foot to type, write with a pen and pick things up between his toes.

Nick's positive attitude and unwavering faith in God have been the driving forces behind his success. He is a firm believer in the power of positive thinking, and he encourages others to focus on their abilities rather than their disabilities. In his speeches, Nick shares his personal story and offers practical advice on how to overcome obstacles, find purpose, and live a life filled with joy and happiness.

Nick has written several books, including *Life Without Limits: Inspiration for a Ridiculously Good Life*, in which he shares his personal experiences and insights on how to overcome adversity and achieve one's goals. He has also established a non-profit organization called Life Without Limbs, which aims to inspire and encourage individuals with disabilities, as well as promote disability awareness and advocacy.

He has inspired millions of people to overcome their own

---

[10] Nick Vujicic, "Something More," PixelKensington channel, YouTube, posted May 20, 2012, https://www.youtube.com/watch?v=ev19ygG9oBI.

challenges and to live their best lives. He has received numerous awards and recognition for his work, including the Young Australian of the Year Award, the Golden Key International Honor Society Award, and the National Courage Award.

Nick also has a great sense of humor. In 2008, reporter Peter Overton met Nick, and interviewed him in a *60 Minutes Australia* interview. [11] In the beginning of the interview, Nick is shown diving off a diving board backwards, saying to Peter Overton, "I'm going out on a limb." At another point in the interview, Nick talks about a situation where his "palms were sweaty."

Remember: Nick has no hands.

His website also shows his upbeat style and humor. On the home page, there is a headline that says "Dis-Arming Nick," which is his "about" section.

Another video shows Nick Vujicic giving a talk in India titled "Reach Beyond Your Goal." Nick states that "when I first met my wife in 2010 it was love at first sight . . . I couldn't feel my legs." [12] The audience didn't laugh, so Nick had to reiterate, "You can laugh. It was a joke. I have no legs." He goes on in the video about valuing yourself, and how his parents told him to focus on what he had—a brain—and not to focus on what he did not have.

---

[11] "No Limbs, No Limits" Inspiring man born without arms or legs – Nick Vujicic, 60 Minutes Australia, posted Sept. 27, 2018, https://www.youtube.com/watch?v=t-JnJ_fTYofQ

[12] "Reach Beyond Your Goal," IDream Teluga Movies channel, YouTube, posted on January 23, 2023, https://www.youtube.com/watch?v=RvPAIo9p8mM.

He states how he is grateful for his beautiful wife and four children, but he was also happy being single, and that this is important to note, even though he is happier married. He speaks about many issues affecting how people view themselves in his motivational talks and addresses bullying in schools where he speaks to students.

Nick's story is a powerful reminder that even the most inspiring and successful people can struggle with depression and suicidal thoughts. However, Nick's experience also shows that it is possible to overcome these challenges and find hope and meaning in life. By sharing his story, Nick has helped many others who may be going through similar struggles, and he continues to inspire and encourage others to never give up, no matter how difficult the journey may be.

Find out more information at https://nickvujicic.com.

Whoa! Enough! Although you have shown me stories of some everyday people, these other people are not your everyday people like you and me! It seems that after going through their terrible ordeals, they become worldwide motivational speakers and stars, like Nick Vujicic and Joni Eareckson Tada. I'm not like that! Besides, I've known several people of faith, and they're not the nicest people on my block. I've seen a bunch of hypocrisy, for sure!

I totally understand, and what I've come to learn is that no matter what a person believes, no matter what worldview or faith they hold, being human also means that we have the free will to choose how to act and how to respond to things, how to talk to people and to be neighborly or not, and that also means the choice to choose good or evil.

To quote from Viktor Frankl's book *Man's Search for Meaning*:

Our generation is realistic, for we have come to know man as he really is. After all, man is that being who invented the gas chambers of Auschwitz; however, he is also that being who entered those gas chambers upright, with the Lord's Prayer or the Shema Yisrael on his lips. [13]

Things to think about:

1. What was the broken pottery in the story?

2. What shattered it?

3. What is the gold filling?

4. What is the lesson and the transformation?

---

[13] Viktor Frankl, *Man's Search for Meaning* (Boston: Beacon Press, 2006) 134.

From Teen Mother to Media Superstar

Oprah Winfrey

Born to an unwed teenage mother, Oprah spent the first six years of her life on her grandmother's farm while her mother looked for work in the north. Life on the farm was primitive, but her grandmother taught her to read very early, and Oprah enjoyed the loving support of her grandmother and church community. Her world changed for the worse at six, when she went to live with her mother, who worked as a housemaid in Milwaukee.

In the long days when her mother was absent from their inner–city apartment, she was repeatedly molested by male relatives and a family friend from the ages of nine to thirteen. She tried to run away and was sent to a juvenile detention home, only to be denied because all the beds were filled. At fourteen, she was out of the house and on her own. She then gave birth to her baby boy when she was fourteen, but her newborn child died shortly after he was born. It wasn't until her mother sent her to live with her father in Nashville, Tennessee, that her life turned around for the better.

According to a *Washington Post* article, Oprah shared, "If I hadn't been sent to my father (when I was 14), I would have gone in another direction. I could have made a good criminal." She recalled how her father was a strict and constant presence in his daughter's life, as was the church. Her father was also very strict about education, encouraging her to get high grades in school.

Oprah is still enjoying an amazing career and has won many awards. However, she still had to overcome another setback that became her tremendous opportunity.

According to Heart radio, "Before she became the star of daytime TV, Oprah Winfrey was fired from her job as an evening news reporter at Baltimore's WJZ–TV because she was 'unfit for television news' and couldn't sever her emotions from her stories. She was given a daytime TV show as a consolation and found her true calling." [14]

Here is a list of some of her most notable accomplishments:

1. She became the first African American female billionaire in North America.

2. She hosted the highly popular talk show *The Oprah Winfrey Show* for twenty–five seasons.

---

[14] "Oprah Winfrey," in "10 Stars Who Were rejected Before Making it Big," Heart, accessed March 8, 2023, http://www.heart.co.uk/showbiz/10-stars-who-were-reject-ed-before-making-it-big/oprah-winfrey/.

3. She founded the media company Harpo Productions.

4. She founded and chaired the Oprah Winfrey Leadership Academy for Girls in South Africa.

5. She established the Oprah Winfrey Foundation to support educational and charitable causes.

6. She's won numerous awards, including nineteen daytime Emmy awards and the Presidential Medal of Freedom.

7. She produced and acted in several successful films, including *The Color Purple* and *Beloved.*

8. She launched Oprah's Book Club, which has had a significant impact on the publishing industry.

9. She became a philanthropist, supporting various causes such as education and disaster relief efforts.

10. She advocates for social justice issues and uses her platform to promote equality and empowerment for marginalized communities.

You are not your circumstances. You are your possibilities. If you know that, you can do anything.

- Oprah Winfrey [15]

---

[15] "Building a Dream," O, The Oprah Magazine, January 2007, https://www.oprah.com/entertainment/building-a-dream (slide 8).

Things to think about:

1. What was the broken pottery in the story?

2. What shattered it?

3. What is the gold filling?

4. What is the lesson and the transformation?

Bringing Light to the World

Thomas Edison

Thomas Edison was one of the most renowned inventors and scientists of the nineteenth and twentieth centuries. He is best known for inventing the incandescent light bulb and for his pioneering work in the field of electrical power generation. However, what many people don't know is that Edison's road to success was not easy, and he faced many obstacles and challenges along the way.

One of the most significant challenges he faced was in the early years of his education. When he was just seven years old, he was expelled from school because his teacher deemed him to be "too stupid to learn anything." The teacher wrote a letter to Edison's mother informing her of the situation and advising her to keep him at home instead of sending him to school. However, instead of giving up on her son, Edison's mother took a different approach. She told him that the letter said he was a genius, and that the teacher didn't understand his unique way of learning.

This pivotal moment in Edison's life had a profound impact on him. Instead of feeling defeated and giving up, he was inspired and motivated to prove the teacher wrong. He started to educate himself and to develop a love for learning. Edison's mother encouraged his curiosity and thirst for knowledge, and he quickly became a voracious reader, devouring books on a wide range of subjects, including science, history, and mathematics. He also began to experiment with various scientific and technological projects, developing an innate understanding of how things worked.

His determination and drive to succeed eventually led him to become one of the most successful inventors of all time. He went on to hold more than one thousand patents and to make numerous scientific and technological breakthroughs that changed the world forever. He proved that intelligence and ability are not fixed traits but can be developed and improved with effort and hard work.

However, one of the most significant adversities that Edison faced was his hearing loss. He was deaf in one ear from a young age and became completely deaf in his later years. Despite this challenge, Edison never let it hold him back. He continued to work tirelessly on his inventions, often working for hours on end in his laboratory. He used his deafness to his advantage, saying that it allowed him to concentrate better and tune out distractions.

Another adversity that Edison faced was the lack of financial support for his inventions. He was often rejected by investors who saw his ideas as too unconventional and risky. However, he never gave up. He continued to work on his projects and eventually succeeded in finding the support he needed to bring his inventions to life.

Edison also faced criticism and skepticism from the scientific community. Many of his contemporaries did not believe in his ideas and thought that he was wasting his time. However, Edison remained undeterred. He believed in himself and his ideas, and he was willing to take risks and pursue his passions no matter what others thought. This determination and self-belief eventually paid off as he went on to change the world with his inventions.

He faced numerous setbacks and failures in his work. He is famously quoted as saying, "I have not failed. I've just found 10,000 ways that won't work." (He was referring to his 10,000 attempts in his quest to invent the light bulb.) What if he had given up after 250 tries, 8,502 tries, or 9,999 tries? He continued to experiment and iterate until he found a solution that worked. This persistence and determination ultimately allowed him to overcome adversity and achieve great success.

Edison was born in a time when electricity was just a spark in the dark, and he was determined to make it a household name. This meant going against the conventional wisdom of his time, which was that electricity was too dangerous for everyday use. But Edison was never one to shy away from a challenge, so he got to work in his laboratory, plugging away at his invention.

One of the biggest obstacles he faced was the naysayers who told him that electricity was just a passing fad and that it would never catch on. But Edison was a man who always kept his eye on the prize, and he was not deterred by these critics. He continued to work tirelessly, testing, and experimenting with different materials until he finally succeeded in inventing the light bulb.

But Edison's troubles didn't stop there. He also had to overcome the challenge of getting people to use his invention. You see, back in those days, people were used to lighting their homes with gas lamps, and they were reluctant to change. But Edison was a master of marketing, and he knew that if he wanted to make the light bulb a household name, he would have to show people its benefits. So, he set up demonstrations, showing people how much brighter and safer his light bulb was compared to the gas lamps they were used to.

And, of course, there was the little matter of electricity not yet being widely available. But Edison was always one step ahead. He saw the potential in this new source of energy and started building power plants to provide electricity to homes and businesses. He knew that if he could get people hooked on electricity, they would never go back to gas lamps. And he was right. Today, electricity is an essential part of our daily lives, and we have Thomas Edison to thank for it.

His story is an inspiring reminder that we should never give up on our dreams or our abilities, no matter what others may say. Edison's mother's faith in him and her belief that he was a genius helped to unleash his full potential, and he went on to achieve great things. This story also highlights the importance of having a supportive and encouraging environment, as well as the power of self-education and self-discovery.

Thomas Edison was a man who faced many adversities in his quest to bring light to the world. But he never let those obstacles get in his way. He took them and turned them into opportunities, and he never stopped until he succeeded. His story serves as a powerful reminder that with hard work and determination, anything is possible.

Opportunity is missed by most people because it is dressed in overalls and looks like work.

-Thomas Edison [16]

Things to think about:

1. What was the broken pottery in the story?

2. What shattered it?

3. What is the gold filling?

4. What is the lesson and the transformation?

---

[16] "Thomas Edison Biography," The Biography.com website, A&E Television Networks, last updated May 13,2021, https://www.biography.com/inventors/thomas-edison.

IT WAS CADET BONEHEAD

By Max James

Reprinted with permission from Max James, *The Harder I Fall
the Higher I Bounce,* (Made for Success Publishing, 2021).

There were lots of lessons learned at the Air Force Academy.
But the one that has served me best came with a heavy load
of emotional grief.

My last semester at the academy, I was the Squadron
Commander for "Fighting Fourth Squadron." Each of the 24
squadrons had an officer that was responsible for monitoring
and assisting the leadership in each squadron. Their title was
Air Force Commander (AOC). Unfortunately, the AOC assigned
to our squadron was a Marine aviator with the rank of major.
He did not want to be at the Air Force Academy. He was
sure it was a very bad blotch on his career progression in
the Marine Corps. He didn't like nor appreciate the Air Force
organization, including the squadron that I commanded. He

chose to show off his preferred Marine Corps training and insist that we learn his Marine ways.

One morning after reveille, with everyone reporting "present" in the hallways, I went back into my quarters to get dressed for assembly and leading the squadron in marching to breakfast. I was standing at the sink and had just lathered up for shaving. There was a pounding knock at my door, and when I opened it, there stood the Marine, fully uniformed in his spit-and-polish appearance.

He yelled to me, "Mr. James, do you know what is going on in this squadron?!"

Not happy to see him there while I was rushing to make assembly and lead my squadron to breakfast, I replied in a much-too-sarcastic manner.

"Yes, Sir. The three S's." (For the unwashed, that means showering, shaving, and ... well, you can guess the third.)

"Follow me. Now!"

I wiped the shaving cream off my face with a towel, threw on my uniform bathrobe and slippers, and marched down the hallway behind him.

Standing in an alcove in front of one of the cadet rooms was one of the Doolies in my squadron, dressed in full, Class-A blue uniform. He was standing at attention with his rifle at "present arms" position and sweating like he had just had a sauna.

The Marine AOC asked him, "Mr. Cadet, what have you been doing here at this position?"

"Sir, I have been doing rifle pushups!"

Now, let me clarify here: A rifle pushup is a physical punishment that was not allowed. After several pushups, when the arms might begin to tremble, it was likely that the hands on top of the rifle, which was lying on its vertical edge, would become unbalanced and roll over, smashing the fingers and knuckles. That was strike one! Rifle punishments would result in the upperclassman who gave them out receiving a major "write-up" that came with walking tours and being restricted to quarters.

Strike two was the fact that physical punishments were not allowed to be given during the period starting 30 minutes before a meal.

"And who instructed you to do these rifle pushups?"

"Sir, it was Cadet Third-Class (a sophomore) Bonehead." (Of course, that was *my* name for the third classman.)

"And where is Cadet Bonehead?"

"Sir, I do not know!"

At this point, the AOC reached over and gently opened the door to the third classman's room. And there was "Bonehead" lying in his bed, taking a snooze.

Strike three! All physical punishments had to be monitored and supervised by an upperclassman.

The Marine turned to me, and with a big ugly grin on his face, said, "Well, Mr. James, I suspect we will be seeing you a little later in the day. You can post back to your room now."

So, I went back to my quarters, finished shaving, and got dressed. I marched the squadron to breakfast, came back to my room, and headed off to my first class.

I knew it was going to be a rotten day.

There I was, sitting in an advanced math class of some sort, with my mind a million miles away. I couldn't help wondering when the next shoe was going to drop and how heavy it might be. Maybe it would be a "class-two" punishment, which would entail the loss of a couple days off base leave and privileges, and perhaps even walking a few tours. Marching tours, dressed in full uniform, carrying a combat rifle, back and forth in the same line for an hour had to be the biggest waste of time one can imagine—*especially* when you only have a few hours of rest, entertainment, or maybe catching up on some classwork.

Surely, I thought, *it would not possibly result in a "class-three" punishment!* That would entail hours and hours of tours, plus being confined to your room for weeks ... or even months. Naw! It really wasn't my fault that Cadet Bonehead broke two or three little old regulations. Hell, I wasn't even there. I was simply doing what was required of me, e.g., preparing to be fully in uniform and on time for my duties to lead my squadron as we marched to breakfast.

And then it started. There was a knock on the classroom door by a Chief Warrant Officer (CWO), who was an aide to the Commandant of Cadets, a one-star Brigadier General who was responsible for all cadet activities and military training.

"Excuse me, Sir, but is there a Cadet James in your class?" The CWO asked the captain who was conducting the class.

"Let's see. Yes, I believe there is. Cadet James?"

"Here, Sir."

At that point, the CWO said, "Sir, the Commandant is requesting Mr. James to join him in his office."

Now at this point I'm beginning to panic. *The Commandant? No, not him!*

He was a former hard-ass troubleshooter from the Strategic Air Command with a reputation of "take no prisoners." He thought the only way to train future lieutenants in the Air Force was to grind 'em down 24/7. And to add insult to injury, I had already had an unpleasant experience with him. This Brigadier General already had me in his sights for the next shoot down.

The CWO was accompanying me down the hallway when he asked me to stop.

"Max, the Com is really angry today. I'm doing my best to stay out of his way, so when you get there, I plan on shutting his door and leaving you two alone. But before you go up to the 'Head Shed' (the building where the Commandant's office was located), the Group Air Officer Commander for your squadron (a Lt. Colonel who reported directly to the Commandant), wants you to stop by his office."

This day was just getting worse and worse. This was the officer that the Marine AOC directly reported to. There was no doubt that he had gotten a full report from the Marine.

Lt. Col. Ashmore greeted me with a return salute and asked me to take a seat. He looked like he was deeply contemplating something—maybe my being in terrible trouble was impacting him negatively. What he told me was that the CWO was correct, and the general was indeed in a foul mood. He said I should just imagine I was back three-plus years as a Doolie, stand fully at attention, run my chin in, and try to just answer "Yes, Sir" and "No, Sir" and "No excuse, Sir."

He also instructed me to come back to his office when the general had finished with me. And with a serious grin, he said, "Good luck!"

As I posted into the Commandant's office and gave the best salute I knew how (after all, I had practiced that salute for four years), he began to talk. Actually, I don't think anyone would have characterized it as "talk." Screaming is probably too drastic a description also, but I suppose yelling is accurate!

"Mr. James, you have obviously lost control of your squadron! One of your men committed three punishable offenses against another cadet. That cadet who broke these regulations put that Doolie in harm's way. And that cadet is your personal responsibility. He is under your chain of command. As the Squadron Commander, it is your job to ensure that all of your men are protected. You have a chain of command under your leadership who are all responsible for those under their command."

And then his voice became even louder as he hollered, "Do you understand me?!"

I did, and I replied appropriately with the only answer acceptable: "Yes, Sir!" But I was not very loud.

"What did you say, James? I'm not sure I understood you!"

"Yes, Sir," I again replied, but this time somewhere just below a yell.

"In your position as a Squadron Commander, you have broken several regulations yourself. And that demands that you pay for your incompetence." The general then yelled for his "assistant"—the CWO who had escorted me from the classroom—to get into his office and look through the Cadet Regulations Manual to find the appropriate regulations and punishments that applied to my situation. The CWO began to leaf quickly through the pages but had no luck finding the regulations the Commandant was needing.

With very little patience, something that this Commandant had never been known for, he began yelling at the CWO.

"What is your problem? Give me the damn manual!"

He also had no success in finding regulations that applied to my situation. The reason is, there were none! Failure in a cadet command position, except in illegal situations, was punishable by a reduction in rank. With his anger increasing in every page he turned, unsuccessfully finding what he wanted, he finally threw the manual back at the CWO and said, "Never mind! Here are your punishments!"

"As a start, you are hereby reduced from the rank of Cadet Lt. Colonel to Cadet First Class. Furthermore, you are stripped of all 'privileges and rewards' you have earned by your having received the designations of Dean's List, Commandant's List, and Superintendent's List. That means you are now restricted to your cadet quarters, and I want you to immediately move out of your room in the squadron area. In fact, find an area that is isolated from the entire cadet wing and move there. No roommate!"

"You will not leave that room except for required academic and athletic classes and events, meals, and other wing formations. In fact, you will now not march as the Squadron Commander at the head of your squadron, but you will march as the last man at the very back of your squadron. And you will turn in your Cadet First-Class sabre and be issued a rifle like all the lower classes of cadets carry for all marching events. And this reduction in rank and command will be announced to the entire cadet wing at this evening's meal formation in the dining room. Now, Cadet James, are we clear?"

"Yes, Sir."

And with that I offered a rather sorry salute, did an about-face, and left his office. My uniform was soaking wet, and my hair was starting to curl. And now I had to face the music again in the AOC's office, as ordered. *Would this day ever end?*

As I returned to the Group AOC's office and was escorted in,

I saluted him and, at his request, took a seat.

"Well, Max, how did it go? Not too well, I would assume?"

So, I filled him in on the session with the Commandant, relaying as best I could remember all of the verbal punishments that had been laid upon me.

"Pretty rough," he said. "I want to share a personal story."

"When I was in the China-Burma-India Theater in WWII, I was a Squadron Commander of a fighter squadron. Two new wet-behind-the-ears lieutenants, fresh out of pilot training, were assigned to my squadron. After one of their early missions, instead of immediately landing (preserving scarce fuel and maintenance supplies), they decided to practice a few aerial combat maneuvers, a friendly dogfight. When they landed, I called them on the carpet and chewed them up one side and down the other. But a few missions later, they repeated their air combat antics. They flew into each other, a midair crash, destroying two critically important fighter aircraft and ending the lives of two important warriors."

"As a result of that happening in my squadron, I was recalled from the war zone to the Pentagon, never to experience aerial combat again. And that is the reason that I have this silver leaf on my shoulder and not something of higher rank."

And then he gave me this leadership principle: You can delegate authority, but you cannot delegate responsibility.

That is the most important lesson I learned at the Academy in all of my four years there. And I have used that principle in all of my companies and other leadership positions I have had. Sometimes the lessons we learn are painful ones. It was humiliating to have my demotion and punishments read to all of the cadet wing. However, that pain was well worth the rewards that this principle has brought me throughout my career.

Oh, and by the way, Lt. Col Ashmore was able to reinstate all my privileges as a First Classman on the various achievement lists. My only responsibilities for the rest of the second semester were to pass academics and take my privileges earned by achieving the requirements to be recognized on the Dean's List, the Commandant's List (isn't that ironic!), and the Superintendent's List.

This great mentor also reinstated me to Cadet Lieutenant Colonel for all the June Week graduation ceremonies and placed me back on the First Group Staff.

That reinstatement also allowed me to receive the "Eagle and Fledglings" award as a Distinguished Graduate at the Graduation Award Ceremony.

Find more information on Max James at https://www.maxjamesauthor.com.

Things to think about:

1. What was the broken pottery in the story?

2. What shattered it?

3. What is the gold filling?

4. What is the lesson and the transformation?

KEEP YOUR EYE ON THE BALL

Michael Jordan

In an Alpha Aspiration interview with Michael Jordan,[17] Jordan stated that he did not start out chasing the dream of playing basketball. He said, "I have envisioned myself playing as a kid, playing professional baseball because I started baseball when I was six years old, and I had most of my success as a child in baseball, and I really didn't have my success at basketball until in my later years. I never chased that dream of becoming a professional basketball player or even a professional baseball player."

He added, "I just played the sport because I loved it and because of the work that I put into it. Next thing you know, success was kinda bestowed upon me without me actually chasing it. It just happened; I didn't think I would ever be this successful."

---

[17] https://youtube.com/shorts/yjXHTeuVAzA?feature=share

In fact, Michael Jordan was cut from his high school basketball team when he tried out as a sophomore. This was a major disappointment for Jordan, who had a deep love for the sport and a strong desire to play.

However, instead of giving up on his dream, Jordan used this setback as motivation. He worked tirelessly to improve his game, practicing for hours every day. He focused on his weaknesses and pushed himself to become a better player. He was determined to prove to his coach and his doubters that he had what it took to play at a high level.

His hard work paid off, as he made the varsity team the following year and went on to lead his team to a state championship. Jordan's reaction to being cut from the team shows his determination and resilience and serves as an inspiration to many people facing adversity in their own lives. He showed that with the right mindset and effort, it is possible to overcome challenges and achieve great things.

Michael Jordan is considered by many as the greatest basketball player of all time. He led the Chicago Bulls to six NBA championships, won five MVP awards, and amassed numerous individual and team accolades.

Jordan had average physical attributes compared to other professional basketball players. He lacked the height of a center, the bulk of a power forward, and the speed of a small forward. However, what Jordan lacked in physical gifts, he made up for in hard work and determination. He trained relentlessly, pushing himself to become the best player he could be. He worked on his shot, his ball handling, and his footwork until he became a complete player.

Jordan also had to overcome adversity in his career. In his second year in the league, he was cut from the USA basketball team that went on to win the gold medal in the 1984 Olympics. This was a major setback for Jordan, but he used it as motivation to become a better player. He worked even harder, focusing on his weaknesses and improving his game.

Another challenge that Jordan faced was losing in the playoffs. Despite being a dominant player in the regular season, Jordan and the Bulls were often unable to make it past the second round of the playoffs. This only fueled Jordan's competitive fire, as he was determined to lead his team to a championship. He refused to accept defeat, and his tenacity paid off when the Bulls won their first championship in 1991.

So, you see, Michael Jordan's road to greatness was not paved with talent alone. Through hard work and determination, Jordan became a complete player, leading the Bulls to six championships and earning a place in the Hall of Fame. With the right mindset and effort, anything is possible.

"I've missed more than 9,000 shots in my career. I've lost almost 300 games. 26 times, I've been trusted to take the game winning shot, and missed. I've failed over and over and over again in my life. And that is why I succeed."

*- **Michael Jordan**[18]*

---

[18] "Michael Jordan 'Failure' Commercial," Scott Cole channel, YouTube, posted Dec. 8, 2012, https://www.youtube.com/watch?v=JA7G7AV-LT8.

1. What was the broken pottery in the story?

2. What shattered it?

3. What is the gold filling?

4. What is the lesson and the transformation?

PILSUNG

By Ron Knueppel of Chung's Tae Kwon Do

It was in college that I discovered taekwondo when I was a senior. I just fell in love with it. It was a three-hour class, twice a week. I found a school in Chicago, where I went to live after college, and took classes there at Chung's Tae Kwon Do, and eventually I became a second-degree black belt.

Several years later, in 1997, as an IT professional, I had an opportunity to move to Anchorage. One day at the end of March, I fell over because I couldn't use the right side of my body. It just stopped working. It was like all the muscles stopped working and my skin had no feeling. And I had this fuzzy line right down my nose. It went straight down my body where I felt one side and had no feeling on the other side. I couldn't use anything. It was completely numb.

I went to Alaska Regional Hospital. They did CAT scans and many other tests to make sure it wasn't a stroke. None of my blood vessels were compressed, and none of them were expanded or bleeding. I was thirty-seven years old. They said, "You know, we don't know what it is, but it's not a stroke." And then I'm pretty sure one night they thought maybe I might be faking. So they were in my room, and I woke up and they were poking me on the right side, with something sharp to see if I would jump. I said, "What are you doing?" The nurse said, "Nothing. We're just checking." They checked everything.

I had work insurance, and I kept my job this whole time because I was on sick leave. I had started the job the month prior to the collapse. My coworkers would come by and visit when I was there in the hospital.

After about a week or two of being in the hospital and having every test imaginable, the medical staff said, "We don't know, but we think you'd do best if we put you in this occupational therapy unit we have here at the hospital."

Shortly after that, my five-year-old daughter was visiting me, and we had a conversation. I told her that I was going to be okay. She said, "I know you'll be okay." I asked her how she knew. She said, "Two angels told me last night that you'll be okay." So, who was I to argue with angels?

After six weeks there, they had run all the tests, and everything kept coming back normal. It's just that my body didn't work. Right about the end of six weeks, the doctor came in and he said, "Well, in my opinion, after all my years of experience, if you were going to be recovering, you would have shown signs by now, so you're probably not going to. So, it's my opinion that you need to sell your vehicle with a stick shift, and you need to get a car that's made for handicapped people. You should plan to be in a wheelchair. You must adjust to the fact that you're paralyzed."

He used this line, "There's still some mysteries of the brain we don't understand. So, I'm sorry, but you're just paralyzed."

The thing is that I had just watched on TV a *Star Trek* episode—this is supposed to be the twenty-fifth or the twenty-sixth century, six hundred years from now in the future—and one of the characters was injured, and the doctor on the show used that exact line. "There's still some mysteries of the brain we don't understand."

Are you kidding? In the *Star Trek* episode, the guy recovered. I thought, "Crap, this is six hundred years in the future, and they still don't know?" But I was mad at the doctor. All I knew was that I had been there for weeks, and they had every test done on me almost every day. They were coming back negative, and they hadn't told me anything. They had no idea what was wrong with me.

But his decision that I was going to stay paralyzed got me very angry. I disagreed and I said, "No, I don't believe you. You can get out of my room—you're fired. I don't even want to see you again." I said, "You get me somebody else."

Well, it pissed me off, so I decided I was going to make my body work. I started with my right thumb, the thumb that didn't work on the table, and I took the left thumb that did work, and I tapped it, then grabbed my right thumb and I tapped it. Then I took that one, put it underneath my right thumb and then tapped it. (I had to have the left thumb holding the other thumb up.)

After a couple hours, suddenly, the thumb could move. Then I worked on the next finger. Physical therapy hadn't done this with me. They showed me how to use the hand that worked, and they ignored the hand that didn't. So, I was making my body move finger by finger. I think I was showing people in therapy, but they didn't change their therapy or acknowledge what I was doing on my own. I got the hand to work. And then I figured out how to make my wrist work, and then I could use that. The therapists were still convinced that the rest of me was going to be paralyzed.

One day, the doctor came back and said, "Oh, so you think you don't need me or you're too good or whatever? Move closer."

By then I was able to stand up on my own. I said, "Look, I can walk. Look at me."

He said, "Oh, you think you're so good." He put this strap around my waist and proceeded to pull me and start jogging with me. "You can't do this," he said.

I had just figured out walking, you know? I stumbled next to him, then he took me back to my room. I was more angry at him now than when he told me I was going to stay paralyzed. I never saw him again.

I think within a week after that I was well enough to go home because I could walk, I could use everything. They did another MRI. The first MRI, I think, was at the beginning of the eight weeks when they were trying to find something wrong. Later, they said that it looked like MS because I had lesions on the brain. It was the first time they found something that wasn't normal. I think that was at the beginning of the rehab stay, not the initial couple of weeks, when they were doing the lumbar puncture and everything else.

Once I was out of the hospital and I had to have a follow up, they did another MRI about six months later. Originally, I had twenty-six lesions on my brain. And then when they did the follow up three months later, I only had six. Usually, they don't go away. The last time I had an MRI was June 2022, and it's still at six lesions after twenty-seven years.

I have been on six different medications over the years. All of them have side effects. The first one, as it was explained to me, was designed to make your body feel like you have the flu so that the white blood cells go out and search for things to get rid of instead of attacking your brain. It distracts them.

After I had my shot, the next morning, I would wake up and it felt like every joint in my body that bent had been beaten up with a stick while I was sleeping; everything that moved hurt. Then I had to do another shot the next day. It was like every other day. I think I was on that one for about three years.

At the end of that, when I stopped taking that medicine, I switched to something else when pills started coming out: there were no pills before that—just the shots. My body had gotten to the point where it hurt on the days when I didn't take my shot. I know I needed the shot to make it not hurt. So then the doctor said my body must be adapting to this, and we have to switch to another medication. I switched medications every few years. One I had to stop taking because it was killing patients in Europe with brain cancer.

One of them gave me what I called man-opause. I would take it, and half an hour later, I would have horrible flushing. My face would turn red. I'd get super-hot and sweaty, and it would last for half an hour. I took that medication twice a day for a couple of years, having those nasty hot flashes; it was horrible. My coworkers used to laugh because my alarm would go off and it was $100 a pill. One would always say, "Oh, there's another hundred bucks," because my alarm went off. And then half an hour later, they'd come by, and it was like menopause. They'd come in just to see me turn red and sweat. This went on for two or three years.

Then some of the medications stopped working. I was told when I was in the hospital that I had what they call "relapsing, remitting" multiple sclerosis, where you get symptoms and then it goes away, and then they flare up again and they go away, and then they come back. Sometimes I would have a relapse, or something didn't feel right or stop working or whatever. Then they'd switch medicines because obviously that one wasn't working.

There was one after that, that kind of scrambled my brain. It wasn't the MS. There were no new signs of anything. But they determined it was a side effect of the medication. I lost all sense of the elapse of time. Everything that was from the past was on a flat window or a flat wall on one side of my brain. And anything I had scheduled for the future was on the other wall and there was no lapse in between.

It's like a movie wheel that went from wall to wall. Everything that happened at any point in the future was the same. It was like in the same plane of existence as anything else. I could never tell the differences of time in the past or the future. When somebody said we must do something next Tuesday, that could mean now, next week, next year, or ten minutes. I didn't know what that meant. It all seemed to me to be the same exact time.

So once that happened, they took me off that medicine and then they put me on the next one. The next one is the one I just finished up with, and it was an injection every six months.

That was better than every day or every other day medicine. This was an infusion: it's like a six-hour procedure, and then it's only every six months.

I was on that one for about five years. The first dose gave me a craving for mint. It always gave me a bronchitis upper respiratory chest infection. That's one of the known side effects. I thought, "Well, alright, it'll only last for a couple of days and then it's done. I'm fine, you know?" But the last dose gave me pneumonia that lasted from January till June.

I didn't do taekwondo for about ten years because of MS. When I was trying to recover, my body just didn't recognize that I had the right side attached. I just couldn't fathom what a right leg meant or right hand meant. It's like having a whole library at your disposal—books or instruction manuals for your body parts—and you open the book up and the pages are blank. You remember you used to have them and how to do the skills vividly. "I used to do that, that's right," but when you try and remember how you did it, all the pages are blank.

Everything that I had forgotten how to do, like walking and running and jogging, I had to relearn, including taekwondo. It's like, "Oh yeah, I was a second-degree black belt when I got MS."

I had to figure out all the forms again, and there weren't a lot of schools available to go to where I live. I started taekwondo again in 2007, about ten years after the MS diagnosis because I had exchange students staying in my home. They saw pictures of me breaking boards and bricks and saw my trophies and they wanted to know if I could teach them some stuff while they were here. I cleared out a chunk of my basement. Then I taught the two exchange students.

Surprisingly, the more I did it, the more things came back, little by little. They liked it. They told their other exchange student friends and then others would show up. So, I had to clear out more of the basement, and soon I had the whole basement cleared out.

Eventually, we had ten or twelve of these exchange students doing martial arts. Then I just decided, "Hey, I want to do this for a business." But before I started, I wanted to be at least a third-degree black belt. I went to Chicago, where my grandmaster was, and I took my belt test there, but our taekwondo school has a rule that if you ask how you did, then you fail. You always have to wait.

I couldn't find out within a week or two how I did, like the other students in the school in Chicago. It was June when I took the test. I didn't know until November when suddenly a box showed up from Chicago that had my black belt in it for third degree, along with a trophy.

Over the next several years, I was promoted up to seventh dan (degree). I am now the Alaska state president of the World Taekwondo Masters Union (WTMU), vice president of the Alaska Martial Arts Association, and the current Alaska state taekwondo referee chairman. I am an experienced referee at the national level, and I have earned both Level 1 Poomsae (forms) and A-1 US referee certification from USA Taekwondo.

I was invited by another grandmaster in Anchorage to speak to his students when he found out I had been paralyzed and had to relearn everything. He invited me to come to his school for one of his black belt events. He said, "I'm so impressed by your indomitable spirit because you didn't give up; you taught yourself to walk again. I want you to tell the parents what your life is like now."

One of the tenets of taekwondo is indomitable spirit. There's courtesy, integrity, perseverance, self-control, and indomitable spirit, and there's another word I use in class, *pilsung*. It's a Korean word that means "victory" but not just a victory. It's a great victory. Like the first time that you figure out how to ride a two-wheel bike and the sense of freedom that it gives you, or the first time you figure out you can swim.

I've overcome a lot, and I don't know what's next, but I keep that victory with me and try to convey that concept to my students when I praise them for a job well done or when they conquer a move or concept in class.

I am now sixty-two years old and have been teaching taekwondo for sixteen years. I teach ten classes a week in addition to a full-time IT job. I am very grateful to be able to still take part in this martial art form, and I have been off all MS medication for a year, since the last side effect of six months of pneumonia.

This is taken from the Chung's Tae Kwon Do Institute website:

Many people believe that martial arts is about punching, kicking, and fighting. However, in our opinion it's a terrific way to teach Respect, Perseverance, Confidence, Self-Discipline, Integrity, Leadership, Courage, and a 'Yes, I can!' attitude.

Lose weight, get in shape, learn new skills and self – confidence

– Amazing Awaits – what are you waiting for?

No More Excuses!

Find more information at https://www.chungstkdalaska.com

Things to think about:

1. What was the broken pottery in the story?

2. What shattered it?

3. What is the gold filling?

4. What is the lesson and the transformation?

PURE GENIUS

Albert Einstein

Albert Einstein, one of the most renowned scientists of all time, was once considered to be academically subnormal by his teacher. This statement might come as a surprise to many, as Einstein is widely regarded as a genius who revolutionized the field of physics. However, it is a well-documented fact that Einstein faced many challenges during his early years in school.

He did not start speaking until he was about four years old, which is considered late for most children. This delayed speech development was a source of concern for Einstein's parents, and he was even evaluated by speech therapists. However, he eventually caught up with his peers and went on to become a highly articulate and well-spoken individual.

Einstein's late start in speaking was a unique aspect of his childhood, but it did not prevent him from achieving great success in the field.

From an early age, he was curious about math and science. However, he struggled with traditional academic subjects such as language and history. He was often bored in class and was considered to be a slow learner by his teachers. As a result, he often daydreamed and lost focus in class, which left him being labeled as "academically subnormal" by one of his teachers.

He continued to pursue his interests in science and mathematics. He was particularly drawn to the idea of how things work and was fascinated by the mysteries of the universe. He spent hours reading about physics and astronomy, and he was self-taught in these subjects. As a result, Einstein developed a deep understanding of these subjects that was far beyond his years.

His perseverance and dedication to his interests eventually paid off. In 1905, he published several groundbreaking papers that revolutionized the field of physics. In these papers, he introduced the theory of special relativity, which changed the way scientists understood space and time. An explanation of special relativity is how speed affects mass, time, and space. He also introduced the equation $E=mc^2$, which described the relationship between mass and energy and became one of the most famous equations in science.

His work was so profound that he was awarded the Nobel Prize in physics in 1921. He went on to become one of the most influential scientists of all time, and his theories and discoveries continue to shape the way we understand the universe.

His story is a testament to the power of perseverance and determination. Despite being labeled as "academically subnormal" by one of his teachers, Einstein went on to achieve great success in the field of physics. His legacy serves as an inspiration to us all and reminds us that our true potential is not determined by the opinions of others, but by our own drive and determination.

"Anyone who has never made a mistake has never tried anything new."

- Albert Einstein [19]

Things to think about:

1. What was the broken pottery in the story?

2. What shattered it?

3. What is the gold filling?

4. What is the lesson and the transformation?

____

[19] https://www.brainyquote.com/quotes/albert_einstein_148788

How Photography and the Pika Saved My Life

By Phillip C. Flippo

Just seven months ago, I was walking out of a hospital, a place that had largely been my home for the previous four and a half years. I was finally able to eat, walk, and function minimally enough that I could go home. I had suffered significant neurological damage from arsenic poisoning and during medical testing discovered I also had a debilitating brain tumor. My corporate life, my home life, my social life: all of it ended in an instant.

My wife (Ashana Flippo) and I truly thought the best life I would ever know again would be one of withstanding the very intense head pain and mental confusion I was now stuck with on a day-to-day basis.

I had always loved to cook, so when I got home, I started

sharing my cell phone photos of every meal I cooked to help distract myself. One day, my photos got the attention of a local restaurant, and they asked if I could take photos for their menu, and I was so excited! Not simply because someone liked my photos, but also because someone thought of me as a real functional human being for the first time in a long time.

Ashana and I knew I couldn't just show up with a cell phone (as we would look a tad unprofessional) so we went to Stewart's Photo in Anchorage, and after many hours of hilarious confusion in having camera basics explained to us for the first time, we bought our first "real" camera. This moment, although I could never have known it, would change my life forever. It quickly escalated beyond taking photos of food, and a week after we bought the camera, we took the world's absolute worst photo of a bald eagle, but something about it transformed us. We stared at this horrible photo for hours, discussing the environment it was in and what it looked like and started asking ourselves questions like, "Why does it live here? What is it doing? Wasn't that so cool to see? What else can we see? When can we go out next?" and this became our new life.

I had previously spent an entire lifetime indoors, and now, all I wanted to do, every single day, was to be in nature, learning and observing the wonders of nature with childlike joy. This was a miracle, this was something I could do, this put my pain and suffering out of my mind, this was more healing than any medication or therapy, and I wasn't just withstanding my days, I was enjoying them.

One day I walked into the Bureau of Land Management and asked a park ranger the following very stupid question, "I have lived in Alaska my whole life, but I have no idea where any animals live, or when they do anything. Can you please tell me where all the animals are?" The other rangers that overheard me laughed a little too hard before one of them happily pulled out a map. On this map were several animals on the edges with child-friendly descriptions and arrows pointing to where they live. One of these animals was something I had never seen or heard about before, the pika.

I spent the next three days talking to locals and researching them, where they live, what they eat, anything I could find. Then I would drive three hours out to where they supposedly were, and I spent entire days desperately searching for them in the rock piles. On the last day, for only four minutes, I saw my first one.

If you have never seen or heard of the pikas, they are the world's smallest member of the Lagomorph (rabbit) family. They are about the size of a hamster, are lightning fast, and spend their days collecting colorful mouthfuls of local berries, flowers, and grasses to bring back to their little homes under the boulders to store for winter. They are extremely skittish and are well known for being exceptionally difficult to photograph, so my daily practice with them allowed me to hone my photography skills at a rapid pace.

One of the pikas became increasingly more curious about me and began having regular interactions with me, and on several occasions, he even left flowers at my feet. I started calling this one Hatcher, and he was the first true meaningful wildlife connection I ever made, and it absolutely opened my heart to a level of beauty and happiness for this planet and its many creatures that I cannot easily describe.

I later applied my learnings and found several local colonies in Hatcher Pass, which I spent the entire summer and fall photographing and filming almost every day.

I started sharing my stories, photos, and videos with people all over Alaska and eventually all over the world. Now, just seven months after picking up our first camera, our stuff has been used by large companies and featured in galleries, and we even published our first Pika calendar a few weeks ago.

I was even nominated and voted best photographer of 2022 in the *Frontiersman* Best of Competition, not because I think I am an amazing photographer, but because I think after everything I have survived, I truly love and value not just nature, but all the people I have met and shared my art with along the way.

For more information, visit www.flippophotography.com.

> Special Note: Ashana Flippo is Phillip's talented wife. She is a face-painting artist and the owner and creator of the event company Color Me Fun. She recently submitted two wearable art outfits and headpieces for the Valley Arts Alliance's 17th Wearable Art Show in Palmer, Alaska. One of her pieces was titled "Conquer Death by Giving Life."

This is what Ashana and Phillip wrote for the announcer to say about this piece:

> "If you discover that you're taking more from the world than you are giving back to it, you will likely have more suffering in your life. Using creativity and giving something positive to the world is how you find your way out of depression, make new friends, and even help save you from crippling illnesses or chronic pain. Creating and sharing art, love, and positivity with others is essential to transforming your one life on this planet into your best life. Living will always have its dark times, but you have to know hell to appreciate heaven."

1. What was the broken pottery in the story?

2. What shattered it?

3. What is the gold filling?

4. What is the lesson and the transformation?

TINOGONA – IT IS ACHIEVABLE

Tererai Trent

This is the remarkable story of Tererai Trent, who grew up in rural Zimbabwe in poverty, wasn't allowed to go to school, and was married at age eleven for the price of a cow. She dared to dream her dreams and went on to live them all in a miraculous way—even becoming Oprah's all-time favorite guest!

A video about her on Oprah's website tells the story of how Tererai wanted so badly to attend her brother's school, but only the boys in her village were allowed to attend school. [20] So Tererai learned to read from her brother's schoolbooks and often did his homework. The teacher eventually caught on to the fact that she did her brother's homework. So the teacher begged her father to let Tererai attend school.

---

[20] Information and quotes that follow are taken from "Tererai Trent's Story," OWN, aired May 20, 2011, https://www.oprah.com/own-oprahshow/tererai-trents-story-video.

She only attended two terms because at the age of eleven, her father sold her to be married. She had three children by the time she was eighteen. She recalls how her husband would beat her because she wanted an education.

In 1991, a woman from Heifer International visited Tererai's village and asked everyone what their hopes and dreams were. Tererai told her that she wanted to go to America to get an education. The woman told her that "if you desire those things, it is achievable."

Tererai's mother told her to "write those dreams down on a piece of paper and then bury them, and if you truly believe in those dreams, then you'll see them grow, and grow, and grow."

She added, "Cover those dreams with a rock because that rock will always call you wherever you are in the world." So Tererai wrote down her dreams, placed them in a tin can, and buried them under a rock.

Her mother told her, "You are the last person to break this vicious cycle of poverty, and I want you to do that."

Tererai responded tearfully in the video, "I did it. I did it."

Oprah tells the rest of the story in the video: "Her first dream that she wrote down on that piece of paper when she was a little girl was to live in the United States. In 1998, Tererai moved to Oklahoma with her husband and five children."

"Dream #2 that she wrote down: just three years later, Tererai, after moving to the United States, earned her bachelor's degree in agricultural education."

"In 2003, Tererai's husband was deported for continuing to abuse her, but she still achieved Dream #3—earning her master's degree in just two years."

Oprah finishes her remarks, "And today [2009] Tererai is happily remarried, and before the end of this year, Tererai will have made Dream # 4 that she wrote down also come true: she will be awarded her PhD."

Tererai then comes on the stage, Oprah and Tererai hug, and Tererai tells her that "it has been an amazing journey."

This is taken from Tererai's website:

"Dr. Trent won the 2018 NAACP Award for Outstanding Literary Work (Instructional) for her latest book, *The Awakened Woman— Remembering & Reigniting Our Sacred Dreams*. She is invited to speak all over the world, to share her remarkable story and the valuable lessons she has learned along the way. She was a keynote speaker at the UN Global Compact Leaders' Summit where she used her growing voice to appeal to international businesses to invest in equal access to quality education. Leading the global charge in the fight for quality education for all children and women's rights, Dr. Trent has become a symbol of hope for everyone and living proof that anything is possible. Her favorite motto is 'Tinogona,' meaning, 'It is achievable!' "[21]

Her website is https://tererair.org/.

____

[21] "About," Tererai Trent International, accessed March 8, 2023, https://tererai.org/index.php/about/

1. What was the broken pottery in the story?

2. What shattered it?

3. What is the gold filling?

4. What is the lesson and the transformation?

Something Else to Ponder About Choices

An old Cherokee man is teaching his grandson about life.

"A fight is going on inside me," he said to the boy. "It is a terrible fight, and it is between two wolves. One is evil—he is anger, envy, sorrow, regret, greed, arrogance, self-pity, guilt, resentment, inferiority, lies, false pride, superiority, and ego."

"The other is good—he is joy, peace, love, hope, serenity, humility, kindness, benevolence, empathy, generosity, truth, compassion, and faith. The same fight is going on inside you and inside every other person too."

The grandson thought about it for a minute and then asked his grandfather, "Which wolf will win?"

*The old Cherokee man simply replied, **"The one that you feed."***

Attitude

"Words can never adequately convey the incredible impact of our attitude toward life. The longer I live the more convinced I become that life is 10 percent what happens to us and 90 percent how we respond to it."

"I believe the single most significant decision I can make on a day-to-

day basis is my choice of attitude. It is more important than my past, my education, my bankroll, my successes or failures, fame, or pain, what other people think of me or say about me, my circumstances, or my position. Attitude keeps me going or cripples my progress. It alone fuels my fire or assaults my hope. When my attitudes are right, there's no barrier too high, no valley too deep, no dream too extreme, no challenge too great for me."

- *Charles Swindoll* [22]

Attitude is everything.

A great example of this "attitude is everything" belief comes from Norman Cousin's wonderful book *Anatomy of an Illness*. Norman Cousins was the editor of the *Saturday Review*. In the mid–1960s, he came down with an incredibly painful case of ankylosing spondylitis. He was bedridden and racked with pain. After much suffering, he decided to end all painkillers and check himself out of the hospital and into a hotel room with a nurse.

He went on high doses of vitamin C and had the nurse read funny stories to him. They watched old comedy films and television shows. He found that ten minutes of solid laughter gave him about two hours of drug–free pain relief. Eventually, he became free of painkillers and sleeping pills and went on to be completely cured.

That form of treatment has now been recognized by the

---

[22] Charles Swindoll, "The Value of a Positive Attitude," The Bible-Teaching Ministry of Pastor Chuck Swindoll, posted November 19, 2015, https://insight.org/resources/daily-devotional/individual/the-value-of-a-positive-attitude

American Medical Association as laughter therapy. His book is inspiring, and I read it when I was being trained through the organization World Laughter Tour as a certified laughter leader during my days as a birthday party clown and Toastmaster member.

The greatest force in the human body is the natural drive for the body to heal itself. But that force is not independent of the belief system. What we believe is the most powerful option of all. The control center of your life is attitude.

*- **Norman Cousins,** the author of* Anatomy of an Illness [23]

So, what do I do now?

It's never too late to start over, believe in yourself, work hard, and go for glory!

What is within you is greater than anything outside of you. Most people have been trained to look at their current circumstances to determine what they can accomplish instead of looking within themselves. The word *responsibility* means we all have the ability to choose how we will respond to life.

Thoughts are powerful! Gratitude and giving back are game changers. A quote often attributed to Aesop says, "Gratitude

---

[23] Sebastian Gendry, "Norman Cousins Anatomy Of An Illness," Laughter Online University, accessed March 8, 2023, https://www.laughteronlineuniversity.com/norman-cousins-anatomy-of-an-illness

turns what we have into enough."[24] To practice feeling grateful and appreciative of all of life's abundance is simple, but its benefits can be transformative.

List several things you're grateful for. Truly feel your sense of appreciation and wonder for the many gifts you've been blessed with. Whether it's the air in your lungs, the sunshine outside your window, the love of your family, or a moment you enjoyed—the more you think about it, the more you will find to be grateful for.

Here are some secrets of self-motivation:

- Set goals!
- Stay focused!
- Do not procrastinate!
- Share your goals!
- Stay positive!
- Reward yourself!

Your history does not determine your destiny. What matters is not where you came from—it's where you're going!

Every adversity, every failure, every heartache carries with it the seed of an equal and greater benefit.

*- **Napoleon Hill,** the author of "*Think and Grow Rich*"* [25]

---

[24] "Quotable Quote," Goodreads, accessed March 17, 2023, https://www.goodreads.com/quotes/11438882-gratitude-turns-what-we-have-into-enough-aesop.

[25] Napoleon Hill, *Think and Grow Rich,* quoted in Jim Rohrbach, " 'Think and Grow Tough' – Napoleon Hill on Adversity," Advisor Perspectives, posted April 7, 2020, https://www.advisorperspectives.com/articles/2020/04/07/think-and-grow-tough-napoleon-hill-on-adversity

Fair enough. Let's start with thinking about all the things you like to do, things that make you happy. Think of skills you have that can turn into income, into a job, if you're not working now.

Next, if you are receiving the services of an agency, see if you can volunteer there. Utilize all the help that they offer if you need more stability in your life.

Here's something important for you to do—no kidding—write down or just think of everything that you love about yourself. Perhaps every night for one week, write two things down that you really love about who you are.

You need to remind yourself daily that you have so much to offer the world! You are unique and wonderful, and the day that you arrived in the world is the day that God needed you to be here.

Many of us were taught that taking care of ourselves was selfish. Actually, when we take care of ourselves, we're able to give our best to those around us and the world. When you take care of yourself, you're giving yourself a signal that you're loving yourself. Imagine that you're taking care of yourself with all the love that you give to the most precious people in your life.

There's a common question that if you are in an airplane and you need to put the oxygen mask on, do you give it first to your child in the seat next to you or use it first for yourself?

Many people say that they'd give it to their child first, but in case management training, we learned that unless you help yourself first, you would be unable to help your child a few minutes after. Something to ponder!

Overcoming adversity requires resilience, determination, and a willingness to adapt. Transferable skills can play a crucial role in helping you to achieve your goals, whatever you decide to do.

Whatever you have gone through, or are going through now, has given you more skills to change your life and the lives around you for the better, if you choose to use what you have learned and developed in yourself.

Here are some steps you can take to use transferable skills to reach your desired outcome:

1. Identify your transferable skills: The first step is to identify the skills that you possess that are transferable to your desired career path. This could include communication, leadership, problem-solving, or time-management skills. Write down your skills and think about how they can be applied to your desired outcome. For example, if you have a special needs child, you have developed skills to assist many other special needs children also, as well as their parents!

2. Set achievable goals: Once you have identified your transferable skills, it's important to set achievable goals that align with your desired outcome. This could mean reaching out to people in your desired industry for informational interviews, enrolling in relevant courses or workshops, or volunteering in related organizations.

3. Build a support network: Building a strong support network can provide you with the encouragement, motivation, and guidance needed to achieve your goals. This could include mentors, friends, or family members who are supportive of your journey.

4. Seek opportunities to grow: Taking advantage of opportunities to grow and develop your skills can help you to overcome adversity and reach your desired outcome. This could mean attending conferences, workshops, or courses, or volunteering for relevant organizations.

5. Be persistent: Overcoming adversity often requires persistence and determination. It's important to stay focused on your goals and not give up when faced with obstacles. It may take time to reach your desired outcome, but with persistence and hard work, you will eventually reach your goal.

6. Celebrate your successes: Celebrating your successes, no matter how small, can help to keep you motivated and focused on your goals. Recognize the progress you have made and reward yourself for your hard work.

7. Take baby steps: Don't try to do too much at once to prevent feeling overwhelmed. Any action taken toward your goals and dreams, no matter how small, is a positive step. Do what you can with what you have to work with whenever you can. It's a win-win no matter what!

8. Do you need to forgive someone who has wronged you? Do you need to forgive yourself for any past mistakes? There is a saying that anger, unforgiveness, resentment, jealousy, hatred, or bitterness (you can add any number of negative emotions) is like you taking a poison and waiting for someone else to die. Letting go of your emotional burdens can free you up to take positive action in your life.

(Of course, I'm a total hypocrite here, because even though I know this principle, I usually beat myself up 436 times in regret and angst before I completely let go of a mistake that I made by word or action.)

So just do your best! Being aware of something negative in your life is the first step. Knowledge can indeed be powerful, especially if it means taking positive action.

Using transferable skills to overcome adversity and reach your desired outcome requires a combination of self-reflection, goal setting, support, and persistence.

By following these steps, you can achieve your goals and make a positive impact in your community, whether it be through a new job, a non-profit organization, a ministry, or just helping a friend or neighbor.

When I was a little girl, I sang a popular song for children with the lyrics: *"Row, row, row your boat, gently down the stream. Merrily, merrily, merrily, merrily, life is but a dream."*

Well, it seems that these days, life is but a meme! Not really, but occasionally!

I saw a clever and funny meme recently. It was a picture of a pig, and it said, *"I turn vegetables into bacon. What's your superpower?"*

In many ways, this book is about turning life's vegetables into a gourmet salad, a prime rib dinner, compost for your garden, or whatever new superpower you choose to create.

"Living will always have its dark times, but you have to know hell to appreciate heaven."

- Ashana and Phillip Flippo

ABOUT THE AUTHOR

Hillary Saffran worked in social services for many years in high stress, low paying jobs while raising three children on her own. Hillary had to discover ways to cope with the financial strain and stress-related issues. She became a birthday party clown, ventriloquist, and author, and turned her stress and life challenges into avenues that brought her tremendous relief while simultaneously bringing joy to others. Now also a transformational coach and therapist in her own practice, it is Hillary's desire to share what she's learned in her journey of life with others and to spread some hope and happiness along the way.

To book Hillary for media interviews and speaking engagements, go to hillarysaffran.com. To purchase her other books and products, visit hillarysaffranproducts.com.